SPECTRUM®

Language Arts

Grade 2

Published by Spectrum®
an imprint of Carson-Dellosa Publishing LLC
Greensboro, NC

Spectrum®
An imprint of Carson-Dellosa Publishing LLC
P.O. Box 35665
Greensboro, NC 27425 USA

ISBN 978-1-4838-1208-3

07-207177811

Chapter I Grammar

Parts of Speech

Sentences

Chapter 2 Mechanics

Capitalization

Punctuation

Chapter 3 Usage

Chapter 4 Writer's Guide

Table of Contents Grade 2

A **noun** is a word that names a person, a place, or a thing.

     brother (person)   park (place)   bicycle (thing)

The nouns in the following sentences are in bold.

     The **teacher** gave us **work** to do.

     The **library** is next to the **pool**.

A **collective noun** is a word for a group of animals, things, or people.

     a **herd** of horses   a **deck** of cards   a **troupe** of actors

Identify It

Read the paragraph below. Circle each noun. There are 20 nouns.

     I packed my bag for camp. I packed shirts, shorts, socks, and shoes. I added my toothbrush and a comb. My mom said to bring a hat. My dad said to bring a game and a book. I wanted to bring my cat. My mom and dad said cats do not go to camp. I brought a photo of my cat, instead.

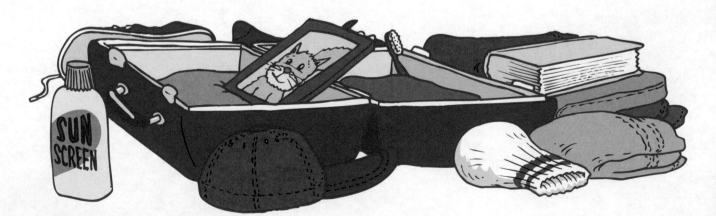

Lesson 1.2   # Common and Collective Nouns

Complete It

A collective noun is missing from each sentence below. Fill in each blank with a noun from the box.

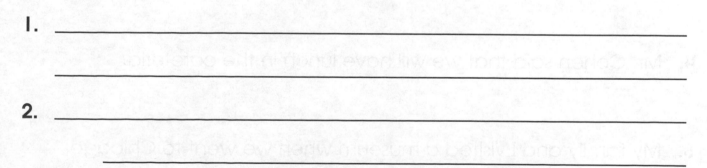

fleet	litter	school
flock	team	pod

1. A _____ of birds landed in the apple tree.

2. Grace's cat gave birth to a _____ of six kittens.

3. A _____ of ships left the harbor at noon.

4. The _____ of hockey players boarded the bus.

5. The shark spotted a _____ of fish.

6. A _____ of dolphins leaped around the boat.

Try It

Write two sentences about what you would pack if you were going on a trip. Each sentence should have two nouns. Circle each noun.

1. _____

_____

2. _____

_____

Lesson 1.2   Proper Nouns

A **proper noun** is a noun that names a special person, place, or thing. Proper nouns begin with a capital letter to show that they are important. Here are some common and proper nouns.

Common Nouns	Proper Nouns
school	Thomas Jefferson Elementary School
sister	Emily
city	Capital City
dog	Bailey

Identify It

Read each sentence below. Underline the nouns. Write the letter **C** above each common noun. Write the letter **P** above each proper noun.

1. The students in my class are going on a trip.

2. We are going to the New England Museum.

3. I am going to sit near Carson, Maddy, and Maria on the bus.

4. Mr. Cohen said that we will have lunch in the cafeteria.

5. My family and I visited a museum when we went to Chicago.

Lesson 1.2   Proper Nouns

Proof It

Read the paragraph below. Remember, proper nouns begin with a capital letter. If they do not, underline the first letter three times. Then, write the capital letter above it.

                 E   B
Example: Max and <u>e</u>nrique went to <u>b</u>uxton Public Library after school.

Chicago is the largest city in illinois. It is near the shores of lake michigan. Aunt suzanne lives there. My sister, ellie, loves to visit her in chicago. They like to go to the museums. Uncle alex said I can come visit next time.

Chicago

Try It

1. Write a sentence that tells about a place you have visited. Your sentence should contain one proper noun. Circle the proper noun.

_____

2. Now, write a sentence that tells about a place you would like to visit one day. It should also tell who you would like to bring along. Your sentence should contain two proper nouns. Circle the proper nouns.

_____

Lesson 1.3   Pronouns

A **pronoun** is a word that takes the place of a noun. Some pronouns are **I, me, you, he, she, him, her, it, we, us, they**, and **them**.

In the sentences below, pronouns take the place of the underlined nouns.

Drew and Lei play softball every Saturday.
They play softball every Saturday.

Dad parked the car in the garage.
Dad parked **it** in the garage.

Reflexive pronouns end in **self** or **selves**.
Myself, yourself, himself, herself, itself, ourselves, and **themselves** are reflexive pronouns.

Identify It

Circle the pronouns in the following paragraph. There are 12 pronouns.

I will never forget the first soccer game I ever saw. Mom, Dad, Laura, and I drove downtown to the stadium. It was lit up against the night sky. We were excited to see the Rangers play. The stadium was filled with hundreds of people. They cheered when the players ran onto the field. Laura and I screamed and clapped ourselves silly. We laughed when the Rangers' mascot did a funny dance. The best part of the game was when Matt Ramos scored the winning goal. He is the best player on the team. It was a night to remember for myself and my family!

Lesson 1.3   Pronouns

Complete It

Read each pair of sentences below. Choose the correct pronoun from the pair in parentheses ( ) to take the place of the underlined word or words. Write it in the space.

1. Mom drove <u>Anna</u> to soccer practice. Mom drove _____ (you, her) to soccer practice.

2. <u>Dan and Marco</u> are on Anna's team. _____ (Him, They) are on Anna's team.

3. <u>Anna</u> kicked the ball out of bounds. _____ (She, Her) kicked the ball out of bounds.

4. The coach talked to <u>the players</u>. The coach talked to _____ (she, them).

Rewrite It

Fill in each blank below with a reflexive pronoun.

1. The team served _____ a snack after the game.

2. Anna cut _____ when she tripped over a rock.

3. Tim blamed _____ for not checking the field better.

4. "You should be proud of _____ for a great game!" said Coach.

Lesson 1.4   Verbs

Verbs are an important part of speech. They are often action words. They tell what happens in a sentence. The verbs in the sentences below are in bold.

Sadie **raced** down the stairs. She **barked** at the cat on the windowsill. Then, she **wagged** her tail at Mrs. Callahan. Sadie **ate** the treat from Mrs. Callahan's hand.

Solve It

Find the verb in each sentence. Write it in the spaces under the sentence.

1. Akiko placed her new puppy on the rug in the living room.

   _ _ O _ _ _

2. The puppy sniffed the rug and the couch.

   _ O _ _ _ _ _

3. The puppy ran in circles around the room.

   _ _ O

4. Akiko and her dad giggled at the excited little dog.

   _ O _ _ _ _ _

5. The puppy chewed on Akiko's green slipper.

   _ _ _ _ O _

What is Akiko's puppy's name? Write the circled letters from your answers on the lines below to spell out the puppy's name.

_ _ _ _ _ _

Lesson 1.4   Verbs

Complete It

Fill in each blank with a verb from the box. Some verbs can be used in more than one sentence.

ran	gave	played
took	threw	chased

1. Sam and Hailey _____ their dogs, Muffy and Baxter, to the park.

2. The dogs _____ in a pond.

3. They _____ around the park again and again.

4. Hailey _____ a stick.

5. Muffy and Baxter _____ the stick.

6. Sam and Hailey _____ Muffy and Baxter two big bones.

Try It

1. What else could Muffy and Baxter do at the park? Write another sentence. Circle the verb.

   _____

2. What do you think Sam and Hailey will do when they get home from the park? Write a sentence. Circle the verb.

   _____

Review

Nouns, Pronouns, and Verbs

Nouns name people, places, and things. Here are some common nouns: **chair**, **tree**, **pillow**, **street**, and **librarian**. **Collective nouns** name groups, like a **colony** of ants, a **forest** of trees, or a **pride** of lions.

Proper nouns begin with a capital letter. They name special people, places, or things. Here are some proper nouns: **United States**, **Uncle Jake**, **Lisa**, and **Mill Street**.

Pronouns can take the place of nouns. These words are pronouns: **I**, **me**, **you**, **he**, **she**, **him**, **her**, **it**, **we**, **us**, **they**, and **them**. **Reflexive pronouns** end in **self** or **selves**.

Verbs are the action words in a sentence. They tell what happens. Here are some verbs: **swing**, **yell**, **fall**, **giggle**, **play**, **ran**, and **smiled**.

Putting It Together

Read the following paragraph. Circle the nouns. Underline the verbs.

Tasha and Sabrina helped their dad all weekend. Dad mowed the lawn. Tasha carried the bag of grass to the street. Sabrina worked in the garden. She pulled all the weeds from the flower garden. She picked the tomatoes, peppers, onions, and beans. Then, Dad, Sabrina, and Tasha painted the garage. After dinner, the girls and their dad had ice cream. The cool treat tasted great after all their hard work.

Review   # Nouns, Pronouns, and Verbs

In each sentence below, circle the common and collective nouns. Underline the proper nouns.

1. Tasha and Sabrina live on Glenwood Avenue.

2. Once, they had a colony of bats in the attic.

3. Their neighbors, Nate, Bryan, and Nikki, live in the gray house across the street.

4. They used to live in Michigan before they moved to Maryland.

5. Nate, Nikki, Sabrina, and Tasha take the bus to Bellevue Elementary School.

6. Mrs. Cullen took their litter of puppies to Miller Vet Hospital for shots.

Circle each pronoun or reflexive pronoun in the sentences below.

1. Nate reminded himself to call Sabrina on Monday.

2. He needed to tell her about a club meeting.

3. It started at 4:00.

4. "We can walk there ourselves," he thought.

5. "I am glad that she and I are neighbors!"

Lesson 1.5 Adjectives

Adjectives are words that describe. They give more information about nouns. Adjectives often answer the question **What kind?**

Kyle has a shirt.   Kyle has a **striped** shirt.

The adjective **striped** tells **what kind** of shirt Kyle has.

The adjectives in the sentences below are in bold.

Linh put the **yellow** flowers on the **wooden** table.
Jess has **curly**, **red** hair.
The **bright** moon shone in the **dark** sky.

Match It

Choose the adjective from the second column that best describes each noun in the first column. Write the letter of the adjective on the line. Some answers can be used twice.

1. the _____ sunshine   a. green

2. the _____ bird   b. rough

3. the _____ grass   c. chirping

4. the _____ squirrel   d. warm

5. the _____ bark of the tree e. noisy

6. the _____ lawnmower   f. furry

Tip Adjectives do not always come before nouns: **The sky is blue**. The adjective **blue** describes the noun **sky**, but it does not come right before it in the sentence.

Lesson 1.5   Adjectives

Identify It

Read the sentences below. Circle the adjectives. Then, underline the nouns the adjectives describe.

Example: Kirsten made some (cold), (sweet) lemonade.

1. A large raccoon lives in the woods near my house.

2. Raccoons have four legs and bushy tails.

3. They have black patches on their faces.

4. It looks like they are wearing funny masks.

5. Raccoons also have dark rings on their tails.

6. They sleep in warm dens in the winter.

7. Raccoons eat fresh fruit, eggs, and insects.

Try It

1. Write a sentence that describes an animal you have seen in the wild. Use two adjectives.

_____

_____

2. Where do you think this animal lives? Write a sentence that describes the animal's home. Use two adjectives.

_____

_____

Lesson 1.6   Adverbs

Adverbs are words that describe verbs. Adverbs often answer the questions **When?**, **Where?**, or **How?**

> She **quickly** opened the umbrella.
> **Quickly** tells **how** the umbrella was opened.
>
> We will go to the museum **later**.
> **Later** tells **when** we will go to the museum.
>
> Maya ran **down** the street.
> **Down** tells **where** Maya ran.

Identify It

Circle the adverb in each sentence below. Then, decide if the adverb tells **when**, **where**, or **how**. Write **when**, **where**, or **how** on the line beside the sentence.

1. Yesterday, it snowed. _____

2. Big flakes fell gently to the ground. _____

3. Ian looked everywhere for his mittens. _____

4. He quickly put on his boots and hat. _____

5. He opened the door and walked outside. _____

6. Ian quietly listened to the snow falling. _____

Tip	Adverbs often end with the letters **ly**. Here are some adverbs: **lightly**, **slowly**, **softly**, **evenly**, **joyfully**, and **loosely**.

Lesson 1.6   Adverbs

Complete It

An adverb is missing from each sentence below. Choose the correct adverb from the words in parentheses ( ). Write it in the blank.

1. Ian _____ ran to his friend Ming's house. (quickly, quick)

2. He knocked _____ at the back door. (loud, loudly)

3. _____, Ming was ready to play in the snow. (Soon, Sooner)

4. Ming's brother, Jin, came home _____. (early, earliest)

5. He _____ joined Ming and Ian in the yard. (happy, happily)

6. _____, they built a snowman. (First, Last)

7. Jin _____ tossed a snowball at his sister. (playful, playfully)

8. Ming, Jin, and Ian went _____ for some hot cocoa. (inside, into)

Try It

Write a sentence that tells about something you did with your friends. Use at least one of these adverbs in your sentence: **slowly**, **quickly**, **loudly**, **quietly**, **easily**, **suddenly**, **before**, **later**, **after**, **sometimes**.

_____

| Tip | When you are looking for the adverb in a sentence, sometimes it helps to find the verb first. Then, ask yourself **When?**, **Where?**, or **How?** about the verb. |

Review | Adjectives and Adverbs

Adjectives describe nouns. Sometimes, they come before the noun in a sentence.

There is a **fuzzy**, **yellow** blanket on the bed.

Sometimes, they are somewhere else in a sentence.

The blanket is **fuzzy** and **yellow**.

In both sentences, the adjectives **fuzzy** and **yellow** describe the noun **blanket**. They tell **what kind** of blanket it is.

Adverbs describe verbs. They answer the question **When?**, **Where?**, or **How?** about the verbs they describe.

Where? **How?**
Kerry sat beside Dylan. The students clapped loudly. They smiled
How? **When?**
happily. Today, their favorite team won the game.

Putting It Together

Read the sentences below. If the underlined word is an adjective, write **adj.** on the line. If it is an adverb, write **adv.** on the line.

1. <u>Yesterday</u>, Carlos and Grandpa walked to the pool. _____

2. The day was <u>hot</u>. _____

3. The <u>blue</u> water was cool to touch. _____

4. Carlos and Grandpa <u>quickly</u> jumped in the pool. _____

5. Carlos loved swimming in the <u>cool</u> water. _____

6. Grandpa <u>easily</u> swam a few laps. _____

Review   Adjectives and Adverbs

Rewrite the following sentences.
Add an adjective to describe each
underlined noun.

Example: A <u>bird</u> sat on the branch.   A **blue** bird sat on the branch.

1. Carlos and Grandpa ate a <u>snack</u>.

_____

2. They sat in the shade of a <u>tree</u>.

_____

3. Later, Carlos went swimming again with a <u>friend</u>.

_____

4. Grandpa read a <u>book</u> he had brought with him.

_____

Read the following paragraphs. Circle each adjective you find.
Underline each adverb. There are six adjectives and five adverbs.

Carlos started to fall asleep on the long, plastic chair. Suddenly,
he heard a loud noise. He felt a drop of cold water on his face.
Carlos thought his friend was playfully splashing him. Grandpa stood
beside Carlos.

"We should quickly find shelter," said Grandpa. Big raindrops
started to fall from the stormy sky. Carlos and Grandpa ran inside.

Lesson 1.7 Statements

A **statement** is a sentence that begins with a capital letter and ends with a period. A statement tells the reader something. Each of the following sentences is a statement.

(M)y brother and I fly kites when we go to the beach.

(M)y kite is shaped like a diamond.

(I)t is purple, blue, and green.

(I)t has a long tail.

Rewrite It

Rewrite the following sentences. Each statement should begin with a capital letter and end with a period.

1. people have flown kites for thousands of years

_____

_____

2. some kites are shaped like dragons or fish

_____

_____

3. others are shaped like birds

_____

4. flying kites is a fun hobby

_____

Spectrum Language Arts
Grade 2
22

Chapter 1 Lesson 7
Grammar: Sentences

Lesson 1.7   Statements

Proof It

Read the following paragraphs. Each statement should begin with a capital letter and end with a period. Use this proofreading mark (≡) under a letter to make it a capital. Use this proofreading mark (⊙) to add a period.

Example: nick and Matt made a kite shaped like a frog .
      ≡

early kites were made in China. They were covered with silk Other kites were covered with paper. the material covering the wooden sticks was sometimes painted by hand

benjamin Franklin did experiments with kites Alexander Graham Bell also used kites in his experiments.

today, kite festivals are held in many cities. people come from all around the world They like to share their kites with other kite lovers. some kites are tiny Others measure as much as one hundred feet

Try It

1. What kind of kite would you make? Write a statement about it.

_____

2. Where would you fly the kite? Write a statement about it.

_____

Lesson 1.8   Questions

Questions are sentences that ask something. A question begins with a capital letter and ends with a question mark.

Ⓦhere are your shoes⑦

Ⓗave you seen my hat⑦

Ⓓid you put my mittens away⑦

Proof It

Read the letter below. Find the four periods that should be question marks. Write question marks in their place.

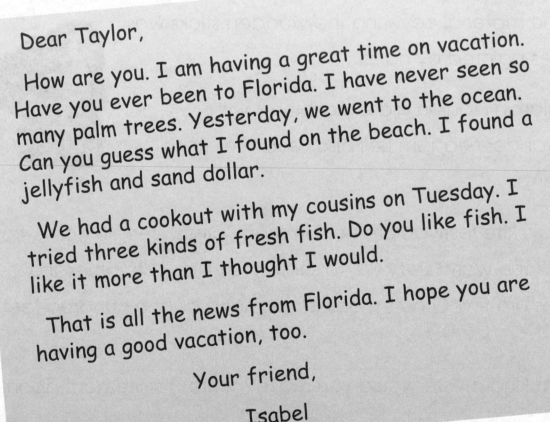

Dear Taylor,

How are you. I am having a great time on vacation. Have you ever been to Florida. I have never seen so many palm trees. Yesterday, we went to the ocean. Can you guess what I found on the beach. I found a jellyfish and sand dollar.

We had a cookout with my cousins on Tuesday. I tried three kinds of fresh fish. Do you like fish. I like it more than I thought I would.

That is all the news from Florida. I hope you are having a good vacation, too.

Your friend,

Isabel

Tip	Questions often begin with words like these: **who, what, when, where, why, how, did, do, will,** and **can.**

Lesson 1.8   Questions

Complete It

Read the sentences that follow. If a sentence is a statement, add a period on the line. If a sentence is a question, add a question mark on the line.

1. Isabel and her family drove to Florida___

2. Do you know how long it took them to get there___

3. They drove for three days___

4. Isabel has two sisters___

5. What did the girls do during the long drive___

6. Did they play games in the car___

7. Everyone in Isabel's family likes to sing___

8. Where will they go on vacation next year___

Try It

On the lines below, write two questions you could ask Isabel about her vacation. Make sure each question begins with a capital letter and ends with a question mark.

_____

_____

_____

_____

Lesson 1.9   Exclamations

Exclamations are sentences that are said with great feeling. They show excitement or surprise. Exclamations begin with a capital letter and end with an exclamation point.

(T)anisha won the race(!)

(I) love your new jacket(!)

(T)here is something scary under the bed(!)

Rewrite It

Rewrite the following sentences. Each exclamation should begin with a capital letter and end with an exclamation point.

1. we won the game

_____

2. maggie hit six homeruns

_____

3. she set a record

_____

4. we are the school champions

_____

Tip	Some exclamations can be a single word. **Surprise! Hurray! Ouch! No!**

Lesson 1.9   Exclamations

Proof It

Read the following diary entry. Find the six periods that should be exclamation points. Write exclamation points in their place.

Tuesday, April 7

Dear Diary,

Today began like any other day. I had no idea what was in store for me. I brought the mail in the house. There was a blue envelope. Hurray. It was just what I had been waiting for. I opened it and pulled out the letter. Here is what it said: Congratulations. You are the grand-prize winner.

I ran upstairs to find my mom. I could not wait to tell her the news. We had won a free vacation. I knew she would be amazed. I enter many contests. I do not usually win, though. What a great day.

Try It

Imagine that you are telling a friend about something exciting that happened to you. Write two sentences that are exclamations. Remember to begin with a capital letter and end with an exclamation point.

1. _____

   _____

2. _____

   _____

Lesson 1.10 Commands

Commands are sentences that tell you to do something. Commands begin with a capital letter. They end with a period.

Do not forget your lunch.   **R**ead the other book first.

Close the door.   **L**ook inside the box.

Statements usually begin with a noun or a pronoun. Commands often begin with a verb. Look at the examples above. The words **do**, **read**, **close**, and **look** are all verbs.

Identify It

Read each sentence below. If it is a command, write **C** on the line. If it is a statement, write **S** on the line.

1. Tia and her grandpa like to bake together. _____

2. They follow special rules in the kitchen. _____

3. Wash your hands after you touch raw eggs. _____

4. Be careful when the stove is hot. _____

5. Read the recipe before you begin. _____

6. Measure the ingredients. _____

7. Tia makes tasty oatmeal cookies. _____

8. Grandpa likes to make cornbread. _____

Lesson 1.10 Commands

Complete It

Each of the following commands is missing a word and an end mark. Choose the word from the box that best completes each command. Then, add the correct end mark.

Drink	Chop	Put
Fill	Blend	Turn

How to Make a Berry Good Smoothie

1. _____ a banana into small pieces__

2. _____ some berries and the banana pieces in the blender__

3. _____ the blender halfway with milk and orange juice__

4. _____ on the blender__

5. _____ the ingredients until they are smooth__

6. _____ the smoothie from a tall glass__

Try It

Think of two rules you need to follow at school. Write them as commands.

Example: Listen quietly when the teacher talks.

1. _____

2. _____

Review   Sentence Types

All sentences begin with a capital letter and end with an end mark.

Statements are sentences that tell. A statement ends with a period.

> The space shuttle will land at noon.

Questions are sentences that ask. A question ends with a question mark.

> What time does the movie start?

Exclamations are sentences that show surprise or excitement. An exclamation ends with an exclamation point.

> There is a shark in the water!

Commands are sentences that tell you to do something. A command usually begins with a verb and ends with a period.

> Bring me two peaches.

Putting It Together

Read the sentences below. Circle the end marks. In the space, write **S** if the sentence is a statement. Write **Q** if it is a question. Write **E** if it is an exclamation. Write **C** if it is a command.

1. Aidan looked at the treasure map. _____

2. Walk eleven paces in a straight line from the mailbox. _____

3. Take six huge steps toward the pond. _____

4. Aidan found an empty hole. _____

5. The treasure had disappeared! _____

6. Who could have taken it? _____

Review Sentence Types

Read the paragraphs below. The mistakes in end punctuation are underlined. Write the correct punctuation mark on the line.

Aidan looked around. Was someone hiding behind the bushes. ___ How did the person know where the treasure was buried. ___ Aidan looked at the map. Oops? ___ He dropped it in the mud. When he bent down to get the map, Aidan spotted a clue. There were footprints by the empty hole? ___ Aidan decided to the follow the prints.

He passed the pond! ___ He passed the mailbox. He followed the footprints into the house. Was the treasure thief hiding inside. ___ Aidan opened the kitchen door. Maxwell was sitting on the floor and wagging his tail? ___ He held the bag of buried treasure in his paws. Maxwell was the treasure thief. ___

1. Answer the following question with a statement. What was Aidan looking for?

   _____

2. Write a question that you could ask Aidan about the map.

   _____

3. What do you think Aidan said when he found the treasure thief? Write an exclamation that shows what he might have said.

   _____

Lesson 1.11 Combining Sentences (Nouns)

Sometimes, sentences can be combined.

Bats eat bugs.   Frogs eat bugs.

Both sentences tell about things that eat insects. These two sentences can be combined into one by using the word **and**.

Bats **and** frogs eat bugs.

Here is another example.

Children like to go to the beach.
Adults like to go to the beach.
Children **and** adults like to go to the beach.

Identify It

Read each pair of sentences below. If the sentences can be joined with the word **and**, make a check mark (✓) on the line. If not, leave the line blank

1. Blue jays visit my birdfeeder. Robins visit my birdfeeder. _____

2. Parrots live in warm places. Penguins live in cold places. _____

3. Hawks build nests on ledges. Eagles build nests on ledges. _____

4. Hummingbirds like flowers. Bees like flowers. _____

5. Geese fly south for the winter. Owls do not fly south in the winter. _____

Lesson 1.11   Combining Sentences (Nouns)

Rewrite It

Combine each pair of sentences below into one sentence. Write the new sentence.

1. Herons live near water. Mallards live near water.

    _____

2. Sparrows are mostly brown. Wrens are mostly brown.

    _____

3. Cardinals eat seeds. Finches eat seeds.

    _____

4. Crows are completely black. Grackles are completely black.

    _____

Try It

1. Think of two things that are the same in some way. They might be the same color or the same size. They might eat the same thing or like doing the same thing. Write a pair of sentences about the two things you chose.

    Example: Cats like to be petted.   Dogs like to be petted.

    _____   _____

2. Now, combine the two sentences you wrote into one.

    _____

Lesson 1.12   Combining Sentences (Verbs)

Sometimes sentences can be combined.

    Julia bikes on Saturday morning.

    Julia jogs on Saturday morning.

Both sentences tell what Julia does on Saturday morning. These two sentences can be joined using the word **and**.

    Julia bikes **and** jogs on Saturday morning.

Complete It

Read the sentences below. Fill in each space with the missing word or words.

1. Mom carried out the birthday cake. Mom placed it on the table.

    _____ carried out the birthday cake _____

    placed it on the table.

2. Carmen took a deep breath. Carmen blew out the candles.

    _____ took a deep breath _____ blew out the

    candles.

3. The children sang "Happy Birthday." The children clapped for
    Carmen.

    _____ sang "Happy Birthday" _____

    clapped for Carmen.

Lesson 1.12   Combining Sentences (Verbs)

Rewrite It

Combine each pair of sentences below
into one sentence.

1. Carmen unwrapped her presents. Carmen opened the boxes.

    _____

2. Carmen smiled. Carmen thanked her friends for the gifts.

    _____

3. Everyone played freeze tag. Everyone had a good time.

    _____

4. The guests ate some cake. The guests drank pink lemonade.

    _____

Try It

1. Write two sentences that tell about things you do. Use a different
    verb in each sentence.

    Example: Carmen sings in a choir. Carmen plays the piano.

    _____ _____

2. Now, combine the two sentences you wrote using the word
    and.

    Example: Carmen sings in a choir and plays the piano.

    _____

Lesson 1.13   Combining Sentences (Adjectives)

Sometimes sentences can be combined.

The wagon was red.   The wagon was shiny.

The adjectives **red** and **shiny** both describe **wagon**. These two sentences can be combined into one by using the word **and**.

The wagon was red **and** shiny.

Here is another example.

Danny has a new scooter.   The scooter is blue.

The adjectives **new** and **blue** describe Danny's scooter. The two sentences can be combined.

Danny has a **new, blue** scooter.

Identify It

Read each pair of sentences below. If the adjectives in both sentences describe the same person or thing, the sentences can be combined. Make a check mark (✓) on the line if the two sentences can be combined.

1. Oliver's painting is bright. Oliver's painting is cheerful. _____

2. Oliver painted the flower garden. The garden was colorful. _____

3. Oliver's paintbrush is soft. Oliver's paints are new. _____

4. The wall is large. The wall is white. _____

5. The tulips are red. The rosebushes are big. _____

Lesson 1.13　Combining Sentences (Adjectives)

Rewrite It

Combine each pair of sentences below into one sentence.

1. The paints are shiny. The paints are wet.

   _____

2. The afternoon is warm. The afternoon is sunny.

   _____

3. Oliver's paintings are beautiful. Oliver's paintings are popular.

   _____

4. The red tulips are Oliver's favorite. The tulips are pretty.

   _____

Try It

1. Write two sentences that describe your hair. Use a different adjective in each sentence.

   Example: My hair is red.　　My hair is curly.

   _____　　_____

2. Now write a sentence that combines the two sentences you wrote.

   Example: My hair is red and curly.

   _____

Review   # Combining Sentences

Sentences can be combined when they tell about the same thing.

Fish live in the ocean.	Dolphins live in the ocean.

Fish and dolphins live in the ocean.

Jackson plays hockey.	Jackson sings in a band.

Jackson plays hockey and sings in a band.

The road is bumpy.	The road is rocky.

The road is bumpy and rocky.

The fast girl is Carla.	The tall girl is Carla.

The fast, tall girl is Carla.

Putting It Together

Read the sentences below. Fill in each blank with the missing word.

1. Luke hiked on the trail. Clara hiked on the trail.

   Luke _____ Clara hiked on the trail.

2. The winding trail led to the top of the mountain. The trail was steep.

   The steep, _____ trail led to the top of the mountain.

3. Luke was tired. Luke was thirsty.

   Luke was tired _____ thirsty.

4. Clara sat on a rock. _____ rested on a rock.

   Clara sat and rested on a rock.

Review   # Combining Sentences

Combine each pair of sentences into one sentence. Write the new sentence on the line.

1. Luke held the wrinkled map.
   The map was damp.

   _____

   _____

2. Luke looked at the map. Clara looked at the map.

   _____

3. A family of hikers passed Luke and Clara. A family of hikers said "hello."

   _____

   _____

4. The family knew a shorter trail. The trail was easier.

   _____

5. Luke smiled. Luke gave the family some apples.

   _____

6. Everyone picked up their bags. Everyone began to hike again.

   _____

   _____

All sentences begin with a capital letter. A capital letter is a sign to the reader that a new sentence is starting.

(M)arisol colored the leaves with a green crayon.
(A)lexander loves to dance.

(T)he bus will arrive at three o'clock.
(I)s the book on the coffee table?

(I) love your backpack!
(R)aise your left hand.

Proof It

Read the paragraphs below. The first word of every sentence should begin with a capital letter. To show that a letter should be a capital, underline it three times (≡). Then, write the capital letter above it.

Y
Example: your socks don't match.
≡

tree trunks can tell the story of a tree's life. a slice of a tree trunk shows many rings. a tree adds a new ring every year. each ring has a light part and a dark part. when scientists look at the rings, they learn about the tree.

the rings can tell how old a tree is. they can tell what the weather was like. if there was a fire or a flood, the rings will show it. trees cannot talk, but they do tell stories.

Lesson 2.1   # Capitalizing the First Word in a Sentence

Rewrite It

Rewrite each sentence below. Make sure
your sentences begin with a capital letter.

1. the oldest living tree is in California.

   _____

2. it is located in the White Mountains.

   _____

3. the tree is more than 4,600 years old.

   _____

4. scientists named the tree Methuselah.

   _____

5. would you like to visit this tree one day?

   _____

Try It

1. Write a sentence about something very old. Be sure to start your
   sentence with a capital letter.

   _____

2. Write a sentence that explains one reason you like trees. Be sure
   to start your sentence with a capital letter.

   _____

Lesson 2.2 — Capitalizing Names

The **name of a person or a pet** always begins with a capital letter.

(J)asper is (E)mily's brother.

The baby polar bear's name is (A)rthur.

Mom always buys (S)niffy's tissues.

Complete It

Complete each sentence below. Write
each name in parentheses ( ). Remember
to capitalize the names of people, pets, and
products.

1. _____ (cassie's) favorite food is
corn on the cob.

2. _____ (omar) loves olives and oranges.

3. _____ (peter's) pet parakeet, _____
(prudence), eats _____ (pet food plus) peanuts.

4. _____ (auntie
ann's apple crunch) is _____ (amy's) favorite cereal.

5. _____ (bradley's) bunny, _____ (boris), eats
beets.

6. _____ (tess) and _____ (tom) like
_____ (tito's tasty tacos).

Lesson 2.2   ## Capitalizing Names

Proof It

Read the paragraph below. The names of people, pets, and products should begin with a capital letter. To show that a letter should be capital, underline it three times (≡). Then, write the capital letter above it.

The neighborhood was getting ready to have a pet show. Geoffrey and gina brushed their pet gerbil, george, with a groom-easy brush they bought at the pet store. hank and harry's hamster, hilda, was ready to perform all her tricks. Sandeep tightly held his snake, simon. The show was ready to start. Only frances and her flamingo, Flora, were still missing. frances had to finish giving flora a bath with clean critters shampoo. Finally, they arrived. The pet show could begin!

Try It

1. Write a sentence using the names of three of your friends.

_____

2. Imagine you had one of the following pets: a hippo, a lion, a whale, a bear, or an anteater. Write a sentence about what you would name your pet.

_____

Lesson 2.3   Capitalizing Titles

A **title** is a word that comes before a person's name. A title gives more information about who a person is. Titles that come before a name begin with a capital letter.

Grandma Sheryl   Uncle David
Cousin Ella   President George Washington
Doctor Wright   Judge Thomas

Titles of respect also begin with a capital letter. Here are some titles of respect: **Mr.**, **Mrs.**, **Ms.**, and **Miss.**

Mr. Garza   Miss Sullivan   Ms. Romano   Mrs. Chun

Proof It

Read the diary entry below. All titles should begin with a capital letter. To show that a letter should be a capital, underline it three times (≡). Then, write the capital letter above it.

Dear Diary,

     Last night, I went to a play with aunt Sonia and uncle Pat. I sat next to cousin Fiona and cousin Nora. The play was about ms. Amelia Earhart, the first woman to fly across the Atlantic Ocean alone. ms. Earhart led an exciting life. She even met president Roosevelt.

     After the play, I met Aunt Sonia's friend, mrs. Angley. She played the role of ms. Earhart. I also met mr. Roche. He played the role of president Roosevelt. He was very kind and funny.

Lesson 2.3   Capitalizing Titles

Rewrite It

Rewrite each of the following sentences.
Remember, titles begin with a capital letter.

1. ms. Earhart lived an exciting life.

    _____

2. Her husband, mr. George Putnam, printed a book about her last journey.

    _____

    _____

3. grandpa Leo gave aunt Sonia the book.

    _____

4. grandma Lucy read it last year.

    _____

5. She also read a book about mrs. Roosevelt.

    _____

Try It

What person from history would you like to meet? Use the person's title in your answer.

_____

_____

NAME _____

Review   Capitalization

Review (sidebar)

Sentences begin with a capital letter.

(D)id your write your letter on the computer?

(T)he yellow dress is torn.

Names of people, pets, and products begin with a capital letter.

(M)ichael named his goldfish (C)leo.

(G)avin and (J)ared bought (K)wik (K)lean paper towels.

Titles that come before a person's name begin with a capital letter.

(P)resident Clinton was in office when Mallory was born.

(A)unt Alia is my mother's sister.

Titles of respect begin with a capital letter.

(M)s. Delaney is the music teacher.

(M)r. Ruiz lives next door.

Putting It Together

Read the paragraph below. Find the 11 words that should begin with a capital letter. Underline each letter that should be a capital letter three times (≡). Then, write the capital letter above it.

President coolidge had many pets. some pets were everyday pets. For example, he had a dog named blackberry and a canary named snowflake. others were more unusual. he also had raccoons named rebecca and horace. president Coolidge even had a donkey named ebenezer. mrs. Coolidge must have liked animals, too!

Spectrum Language Arts
Grade 2
46

Review: Chapter 2 Lessons 1–3
Mechanics: Capitalization

Review | # Capitalization

Rewrite each of the following sentences. Remember to start each sentence with a capital letter. Names also begin with a capital letter.

1. president kennedy liked animals.

   _____

2. charlie and pushinka were two of his dogs.

   _____

3. his daughter, caroline, had a pony named macaroni.

   _____

   _____

4. mrs. jackie kennedy had a horse named sardar.

   _____

   _____

Circle the product name in each sentence that should be capitalized.

1. This week, all pet perks products are on sale.

2. We sell less mess puppy pads to help with housetraining.

3. happy cats makes six kinds of treats for your kitties.

4. Do you have a new hamster or gerbil? Check out a rodent ranch pet care kit.

Lesson 2.4   Capitalizing Place Names

The **names of special places** always begin with a capital letter.

Ⓡockwell Ⓔlementary Ⓢchool   Ⓖarner Ⓢcience Ⓜuseum

Ⓞrlando, Ⓕlorida   Ⓑay Ⓥillage Ⓛibrary

Ⓜississippi Ⓡiver   Ⓜars

Ⓓonovan Ⓢtreet   Ⓕrance

Complete It

Complete each sentence below with the word in parentheses ( ). Remember, special places begin with a capital letter.

1. My family left Charlotte,

    _____ (north carolina), yesterday

    morning.

2. We waved good-bye to our house on

    _____ (clancy avenue).

3. We passed _____

    (washington elementary school).

4. Then, we crossed _____

    (hilliard bridge).

5. We were on our way across the _____

    (united states)!

Lesson 2.4   Capitalizing Place Names

Proof It

Read the postcard below. Find the 15 words that should begin with a capital letter. Underline each letter that should be a capital three times (≡). Then, write the capital letter above it.

Hi Annie,

I am writing from arizona. Today, we went to the tucson children's museum. Tomorrow, we will head to the grand canyon. Next week, we'll be in california. We will visit stanford university. That is where my parents went to college. Then, we will head north. I can't wait to see redwood national forest.

Your pal,

Priya

United States
23¢

Annie Schneider

452 cherry lane

charlotte, NC 22471

Try It

1. What state or city would you like to visit? Be sure to capitalize the name in your answer.

_____

2. What school do you go to? Write your answer on the line below. Use capital letters where they are needed.

_____

Lesson 2.5   Capitalizing Days, Months, and Holidays

The **days of the week** each begin with a capital letter.

Ⓜonday, Ⓣuesday, Ⓦednesday, Ⓣhursday, Ⓕriday, Ⓢaturday, Ⓢunday

The **months of the year** are also capitalized.

Ⓙanuary, Ⓜay, Ⓙune, Ⓞctober,

The **names of holidays** begin with a capital letter.

Ⓒhristmas, Ⓣhanksgiving, Ⓥalentine's Ⓓay, Ⓚwanzaa

Proof It

Read the sentences below. Underline each letter that should be capital three times (≡). Then, write the capital letter above it.

1. I have to go to the doctor on monday.

2. Softball practice starts on tuesday afternoon.

3. wednesday is Miguel's birthday.

4. There is no school on presidents' day.

5. I will go to my piano lesson on friday.

6. We will go to the grocery store on saturday morning.

7. Grandma will visit during hanukkah.

Mon.	Tues.	Wed.	Thurs.	Fri.	Sat.	Sun.
1	2	3	4	5	6	7
doctor appointment	softball practice	Miguel's birthday	presidents' day	piano practice	grocery shopping	hanukkah

Lesson 2.5   Capitalizing Days, Months, and Holidays

Rewrite It

The Brandon family keeps a list of important holidays and dates. Read the list. If the date or holiday is written correctly, make a check mark (✓) on the line. If it is not written correctly, rewrite it.

Ella's birthday	january 20	_____
valentine's Day	February 14	_____
Shane's party	May 11	_____
Kahlil's first birthday	june 22	_____
the Cheswicks' trip	july 18	_____
thanksgiving	November 23	_____
Tyson's birthday	december 29	_____

Try It

1. Write a sentence about something that happened this week. Tell what day of the week it happened.

    _____

    _____

2. What is your favorite holiday? Why?

    _____

    _____

Review | Capitalization

The **names of special places** always begin with a capital letter.

(W)estwood Hospital   (B)razil

(L)inden (S)treet   (P)ittsburgh, (P)ennsylvania

(L)ake (E)rie   (H)ampton (H)igh (S)chool

The **names of days, months, and holidays** always begin with a capital letter.

Summer vacation starts on (T)hursday, (J)une 9.

We first met in (O)ctober.

We always have a cookout on (L)abor (D)ay.

Putting It Together

Read the directions below. Complete each sentence with the word or words in parentheses ( ). Remember, special places begin with a capital letter.

- Take _____ (maple street) to _____ (oak lane), and turn left.

- You will pass _____ (wintergreen school).

- Turn left on _____ (westbury avenue).

- In about a mile, you will see _____ (lane pool).

- Turn right on _____ (pine hill drive).

- Cross _____ (stony creek), and continue for two miles.

- You will see a _____ (michigan) flag by the front door of our house.

Review   Capitalization

Read the paragraph below. Underline each letter that should be a capital letter three times (≡). Then, write the capital letter above it. You should find 11 words that should begin with a capital letter.

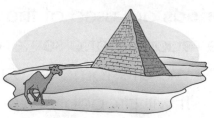

In september, Uncle Jack went to egypt. He got to cairo on a sunny monday morning. He had a long list of places to visit. Uncle Jack went to the museum on tuesday. Later, he took a boat down the nile river. He rode a camel in the desert. He even swam in the red sea. Just before thanksgiving, he flew home to minnesota.

Read each sentence below. If the sentence is correct, make a check mark on the line. If it is incorrect, make an **X** on the line. Then, circle the letter or letters that should be capitalized.

I.   _____   In December, Uncle Jack flew to Paris.

2.   _____   He said he would like to live in france one day.

3.   _____   Then, he took a train to Switzerland for christmas.

4.   _____   He went skiing in the swiss alps.

5.   _____   Uncle Jack called to say happy birthday to me on saturday, march 4.

6.   _____   One day, he will take me to paris, rome, and berlin.

Lesson 2.6   Periods

Periods are used at the ends of statements and commands. They tell the reader that a sentence has ended.

We ate tomato soup for lunch.

It will probably rain this afternoon.

Run as fast as you can.

Kris was wearing a blue baseball cap.

Proof It

Read the paragraph below. It is missing six periods. Add the missing periods. Circle each one so that it is easy to see.

Tip	A capital letter can be a sign that a new sentence is beginning.

Most people do not like mosquitoes If you spend any time outside

in the summer, you will probably get bitten Not all mosquitoes bite

people Only female mosquitoes bite

people When mosquitoes bite, they take

a drop of blood from a person Some

mosquitoes like birds or flowers better

Lesson 2.6　Periods

Rewrite It

Rewrite the following sentences. Each one should end with a period.
Circle the periods.

1. There are thousands of types of mosquitoes

_____

2. Mosquitoes like human sweat

_____

3. Some people never get mosquito bites

_____

4. Mosquitoes lay eggs in still water

_____

5. Bug spray can protect you from bites

_____

Try It

Have you ever been bitten by a bug? Write two sentences about it.
Both sentences should end with a period.

_____

_____

_____

Lesson 2.7   Question Marks

Use a **question mark** to end a sentence that asks a question.

Where did you put the crayons**?**
What time will Grandpa get here**?**
How did you like the play**?**
Did you go swimming**?**

Complete It

Read each answer below. Then, write the question that goes with the answer.

Example: **Q:** <u>What color is the sweater?</u>
　　　　　A: The sweater is yellow.

1. **Q:** _____
   A: I ate spaghetti for dinner.

2. **Q:** _____
   A: My skateboard is in the garage.

3. **Q:** _____
   A: Keiko went to the library.

4. **Q:** _____
   A: Ashton is seven years old.

5. **Q:** _____
   A: Mr. Arnold lives in Houston.

6. **Q:** _____
   A: The book is about a boy who wishes he could fly.

Lesson 2.7   Question Marks

Proof It

Theo is asking an author questions for a school report. Cross out the six wrong end marks. Add the correct end marks, and circle them.

Theo: What do you like about being a writer.

Ms. Loden: I love to tell stories.

Theo: Where do you get your ideas.

Ms. Loden: I used to be a teacher? Many ideas come from the children who were in my classes.

Theo: When do you write.

Ms. Loden: I write for about four hours every morning?

Theo: Do you have any hobbies.

Ms. Loden: I like to garden, ski, and do crossword puzzles.

Try It

What are two questions you would like to ask the author of your favorite book? Write them on the lines below. Remember to end each question with a question mark.

_____

_____

_____

Lesson 2.8 Exclamation Points

An **exclamation** point is used to end a sentence that is exciting. Sometimes exclamation points are used to show surprise.

Look at the rainbow**!**   I loved that movie**!**

Wow**!**   My class got a new computer**!**

Proof It

Read the poster below. Six exclamation points and two periods are missing. Add the end marks where they are needed.

Hurray

THE BELLVIEW FAIR
is coming to town in July

Win great prizes

Ride the biggest Ferris wheel
in Clark County

Sample tasty foods
from around the world

Admission is $3.00 for adults
and $2.00 for kids under twelve

The fair opens July 6 and closes July 12

DON'T MISS ALL THE FUN

Lesson 2.8   Exclamation Points

Complete It

Read the sentences below. One sentence in each pair should end with a period. One should end with an exclamation point. Add the correct end marks.

1. I went to the Bellview Fair__
   I had the best time__

2. I played a game called Toss the Ring__
   I won four stuffed animals__

3. All the sheep escaped from their pen__
   It did not take the farmers long to catch them, though__

4. I ate a snow cone and some cotton candy__
   The cotton candy got stuck in my hair__

Try It

Think about an exciting place you have been. It could be a fair, sports event, field trip, or vacation. Write two exciting things that happened. End each sentence with an exclamation point.

Example: Yea, he hit a homerun! Wow, what a game!

_____

_____

_____

_____

Lesson 2.9   Periods in Abbreviations

An **abbreviation** is a short way of writing something. Most abbreviations are followed by a period.

The **days of the week** can be abbreviated.

Mon. Tues. Wed. Thurs. Fri. Sat. Sun.

The **months of the year** also can be abbreviated. **May**, **June**, and **July** are not abbreviated because their names are so short.

Jan. Feb. Mar. Apr. Aug. Sept. Oct. Nov. Dec.

People's titles are almost always abbreviated when they come before a name.

Mrs. = missus   Mr. = mister   Dr. = doctor

Types of streets are abbreviated in addresses.

St. = street   Ave. = avenue   Dr. = drive   Ln. = lane

Match It

Read each underlined word in the first column. Find the matching abbreviation in the second column. Write the letter of the abbreviation on the line.

1. _____ 19052 Inglewood <u>Avenue</u>   **a.**   Thurs.

2. _____ <u>Doctor</u> Weinstein   **b.**   Jan.

3. _____ <u>Thursday</u> night   **c.**   Dr.

4. _____ <u>October</u> 15, 2006   **d.**   Ln.

5. _____ 18 Winding Creek <u>Lane</u>   **e.**   Ave.

6. _____ <u>January</u> 1, 2000   **f.**   Oct.

Lesson 2.9   Periods in Abbreviations

Complete It

Read each word in parentheses ( ). Write the abbreviation.

Example: Sunday, _____Nov._____ (November) 12

1. 4250 Rosehill _____ (Street)

2. _____ (Mister) Ortega

3. _____ (April) 4, 2014

4. _____ (February) 10, 1904

5. _____ (Wednesday) morning

6. _____ (Missus) Antonivic

7. Beech _____ (Drive)

Try It

1. Write your street address or school address using an abbreviation. Here are some other abbreviations you may need:

   Rd. = road   Blvd. = boulevard   Ct. = court   Cir. = circle

   _____

2. Write today's date using an abbreviation for the day of the week and month.

   _____

Review   # End Marks and Abbreviations

A **period** is used at the end of a sentence that is a statement or command.

My favorite color is light green.   Close the door, please.

A **question mark** is used at the end of a sentence that asks a question.

When did you call Aunt Elaine**?**

What time does the movie begin**?**

An **exclamation point** is used at the end of an exclamation.

Ouch**!**   I dropped the cake**!**   Samir lost the keys**!**

An **abbreviation** is a short way of writing a word. Abbreviations are often used in dates, addresses, and titles. A period usually comes after an abbreviation.

Mon. morning   **Feb.** 14   Locust **Ave.**   **Mr.** Williams

Putting It Together

The sentences below are missing end marks. Read each sentence. Then, add the correct end mark on the line.

1. Thursday started out like any other day__

2. I ate breakfast and went to school__

3. When I came home, my mom and dad told me the news__

4. Do you know what they said__

5. I am going to be a big brother__

Review — End Marks and Abbreviations

Rewrite each item below. Use an abbreviation in place of each underlined word.

1. <u>Missus</u> Lahiri _____

2. 1642 Delmar <u>Lane</u> _____

3. <u>Tuesday</u>, August 2 _____

4. <u>November</u> 22, 2004 _____

5. <u>Doctor</u> White _____

6. 745 San Luis <u>Street</u> _____

Read the letter below. The underlined end marks are wrong. Draw a line through them. Write the correct end marks above them.

Dear Jamie,

How are you<u>.</u> How do you like being in third grade<u>!</u> I am having a good year at school. My second-grade teacher is very nice<u>?</u> He is also funny. He loves to tell jokes and make us laugh. Do you like your teacher<u>.</u>

Guess what<u>.</u> I won the annual Busy Bee Spelling Bee last week<u>.</u> The grand prize was a gift certificate to a bookstore<u>?</u> My parents took me out to dinner to celebrate. It was a great day<u>?</u>

Write back to me soon. I miss you<u>.</u>

  Your cousin,

  Elizabeth

Lesson 2.10 Commas with Dates, Cities, and States

Commas are used in dates. They are used in between the day of the month and the year.

January 11, 1988   October 8, 1845   June 25, 2015

Commas are also used in between the names of cities and states.

Charleston, South Carolina   Bangor, Maine

When the names of cities and states are in the middle of a sentence, a comma goes after the name of the state, too.

After we left Council Bluffs, Iowa, we headed north.

Meghan and Becca moved from Oxford, Ohio, to San Antonio, Texas.

Proof It

Read the words below. Eight commas are missing. Add each comma where it belongs by using this symbol (∧).

Example: Once you pass Huntsville, Alabama, you will be halfway there.

1. Selma was born on August 16 2008.

2. She lives in Taos New Mexico.

3. Her little sister was born on April 4 2012.

4. Selma's grandparents live in Denver Colorado.

5. It is a long drive from Denver Colorado to Taos New Mexico.

6. The last time Selma's grandparents visited was December 20 2013.

Lesson 2.10 Commas with Dates, Cities, and States

Identify It

Read each line below. If it is correct, make a check mark (✓) on the line. If it is wrong, rewrite it.

1. March, 4 1952 _____

2. Butte Montana _____

3. May 27 2001 _____

4. The plane stopped in Baltimore, Maryland, to get more fuel.

_____

5. It snowed eight inches in Stowe Vermont.

_____

6. November 4, 2015 _____

7. Gum Spring, Virginia is where my grandma lives.

_____

Try It

1. Write a sentence about a city and state you would like to visit. Remember to use commas where they are needed.

_____

2. Ask a classmate when he or she was born. Write the date, including the year, on the line below.

_____

Lesson 2.11   Commas in Series and in Letters

A **series** is a list of words. Use a comma after each word in the series except the last word.

>   Mom bought carrots, lettuce, tomatoes, and peppers.
>   Cody's sisters are named Cassidy, Cameron, Casey, and Colleen.

In a letter, a comma follows **the greeting** and **the closing**.

>   Dear Mr. Wong,   Your friend,

Rewrite It

Rewrite the sentences below. Add commas to each list to make the sentences clearer.

1. Mom got out the picnic basket the plates and the cups.

    _____

    _____

2. Lily packed forks knives spoons and napkins.

    _____

    _____

3. Amelia added pears oranges and apples.

    _____

4. Dad made sandwiches a salad and brownies.

    _____

Lesson 2.11   Commas in Series and in Letters

Proof It

Read the letter below. Ten commas are missing. Add each comma where it belongs by using this symbol (∧).

Dear Grandma

    Yesterday, we went to at the park. Lily Amelia and Mom shook out the picnic blanket. Dad carried the basket the drinks and the toys from the car. We all ate some salad a sandwich and a fruit.

    Deepak Sita and Raj were at the park with their parents, too. We played tag and fed the ducks. Later, we shared our brownies with the Nair family. I wish you could have been there!

    Love

    Max

Try It

1. Imagine you were going on a picnic. What three things would you bring with you? Remember to separate the things in your list with commas.

_____

_____

2. Name three people who live on your street or go to your school. Separate their names with commas.

_____

_____

Lesson 2.12 Commas in Compound Sentences

A **compound sentence** is made up of two smaller sentences. The smaller sentences are joined by a comma and the word **and** or **but**.

Michelle went to the store.   She bought some markers.
Michelle went to the store, **and** she bought some markers.

Bats sleep during the day.   They are active at night.
Bats sleep during the day, **but** they are active at night.

Rewrite It

Read the sentences below. Combine them using a comma and the word **and** or **but**.

1. Abby rode her bike. Gilbert rode his scooter.

_____

_____

2. My new bedroom is big. My old bedroom was cozy.

_____

_____

3. The black cat is beautiful. The orange cat is friendly.

_____

_____

4. Roberto is quick. Sophie is more graceful.

_____

Lesson 2.12 Commas in Compound Sentences

Proof It

Read the paragraph below. Four commas are missing from compound sentences. Add each comma where it belongs by using this symbol (∧).

> **Tip** Look for the words **and** or **but**. Ask yourself if they join two complete sentences.

The leaves of the poison ivy plant are shaped like almonds and they come in groups of three. Poison ivy can cause a rash and it can make you itch. The leaves of the plant contain oil that causes the rash. Some people can touch the plant but they will not get a rash.

The oil can stick to your clothes. Washing with soap and water can get rid of the oil and it can keep the rash from spreading.

Try It

Write a compound sentence about what you like to do and what a friend of yours likes to do. Remember to join the two parts of your sentence with a comma and the word **and** or **but**.

Example: I like to play at the park, and Deena likes to go swimming.

_____

_____

Lesson 2.13   Apostrophes in Possessives

When something belongs to a person or thing, they own it. An apostrophe and the letter **s** ('s) at the end of a word show that the person or thing is the owner.

the car**'s** engine   Stacy**'s** eyes

Jake**'s** laugh   the table**'s** leg

Rewrite It

Read each phrase below. Then, rewrite it on the line as a possessive.

Example: the coat of Kayla _____ Kayla's coat _____

1. the roar of the lion _____

2. the spots of the leopard _____

3. the trip of Amy _____

4. the lens of the camera _____

5. the hat of Tim _____

6. the roof of the jeep _____

Lesson 2.13   Apostrophes in Possessives

Match It

Read the words below. Then, read the answer choices. Write the letter of your answer on the line.

1. _____ the horn of the rhino
   a. the rhino's horn   b. the horn's rhino

2. _____ the animals of Africa
   a. the animal's of Africa   b. Africa's animals

3. _____ the photos of John
   a. John photo's   b. John's photos

4. _____ the leader of the safari
   a. the safari's leader   b. the leader safari's

5. _____ the favorite animal of Don
   a. Don's favorite animal's   b. Don's favorite animal

6. _____ the baby of the hippo
   a. the baby's hippo   b. the hippo's baby

7. _____ the tent of Sarah
   a. Sarah's tent   b. Sarah tent

Try It

1. On the line below, write something you like about one of your friends. Use the possessive form of your friend's name.

Example: I like William's smile.

Review   Commas and Apostrophes

Commas are used in between the day of the month and the year.

May 8, 1846   August 19, 1989   February 28, 2003

Commas are also used to separate cities and states. A comma follows the name of a city and state in the middle of a sentence.

Seattle, Washington   Augusta, Georgia   Tallahassee, Florida

A comma follows each item in a series except for the last.

The box was filled with pencils, pens, crayons, and paints.

A comma follows the greeting and closing of a letter.

Dear Will,   Much love,

The smaller sentences in a compound sentence are joined by a comma and the word **and** or **but**.

Andy wrote a letter, **and** Lauren read a book.

An apostrophe and the letter **s** after a word ('s) show that a person or thing owns something.

Jacinta**'s** desk   the tree**'s** leaves   my mother**'s** necklace

Putting It Together

Rewrite each sentence below. Add commas where they are needed.

1. Peter Jenkins travels and he writes books about his adventures.

_____

2. He brought a backpack food and clothes.

_____

3. New Orleans Louisiana was one stop on Peter's journey.

_____

Review **Commas and Apostrophes**

Read the paragraphs below. There are 17 commas missing. Write each comma where it belongs.

Dear Quinn

I need to write a letter for school. I chose to write to you about Peter Jenkins. He was born on July 8 1951 in Greenwich Connecticut. Peter is best known for walking across America. He began his walk on October 15 1973. He walked from Alfred New York to Florence Oregon. His walk ended on January 18 1979.

Today, Peter lives on a farm in Spring Hill Tennessee. His children are named Rebekah Jedidiah Luke Aaron Brooke and Julianne. Peter likes to travel write and speak to people about his adventures.

I hope you liked learning about Peter. I'll talk to you soon!

Your friend

Eli

Read each sentence below. Rewrite the words in parentheses ( ) so they show ownership.

1. (The dog of Peter) _____, Cooper, walked across America with him.

2. (The people of America) _____ are very interesting to Peter Jenkins.

3. (The books of Peter) _____ are about the places he has traveled.

Lesson 2.14 Quotation Marks in Dialogue

Quotation marks are used around the exact words a person says. One set of quotation marks is used before the first word the person says. Another set is used at the end of the person's words.

Jamal said, "I am going to play in a piano recital on Saturday."

"Do you like fresh apple pie?" asked the baker.

"Hurray!" shouted Sydney. "Today is a snow day!"

Remember to put the second pair of quotation marks after the punctuation mark that ends the sentence.

Complete It

Read each sentence below. Underline the speaker's exact words. Then, add a set of quotation marks before and after the speaker's words.

Example: Enzo shouted, "Catch the ball, Katie!"

1. Would you like to go to skiing this afternoon? asked Mom.

2. Alyssa asked, Where will we go?

3. Mom said, Wintergreen Mountain is not too far away.

4. Can I bring a friend? asked Zane.

5. Mom said, You can each bring along one friend.

6. Alyssa said, Riley will be so excited!

Tip	The exact words people say are sometimes called **dialogue**. Quotation marks are used to show which words are dialogue.

Lesson 2.14 ## Quotation Marks in Dialogue

Rewrite It

Read each sentence below. Write the sentence again. Add quotation marks where they are needed. Remember to find the speaker's exact words first.

1. Have you ever been skiing? Zane asked his friend.

   _____

2. Joey said, No, but it sounds like fun.

   _____

3. Riley said, My grandpa taught me how to ski.

   _____

4. She added, He lives near the mountains in Vermont.

   _____

   _____

Try It

Write two sentences that have people speaking. Begin each sentence with one of these phrases.

   My mom said, My friend said, My sister said, My grandpa said,

1. _____

2. _____

Lesson 2.15 Titles of Books and Movies

The **titles of books and movies** are underlined in text. This lets the reader know that the underlined words are part of a title.

Cristina's favorite movie is <u>Because of Winn-Dixie</u>.

Harry wrote a book report on <u>Nate the Great and the Musical Note</u>.

Roald Dahl is the author of <u>James and the Giant Peach</u>.

I have seen the movie <u>Aladdin</u> four times.

Rewrite It

Read the sentences below. Rewrite each sentence and underline the title of each movie.

1. Tom Hanks was the voice of Woody in the movie Toy Story.

   _____

2. Mara Wilson played Matilda Wormwood in the movie Matilda.

   _____

3. In the movie Shrek, Cameron Diaz was the voice of Princess Fiona.

   _____

4. The movie Fly Away Home is based on a true story.

   _____

5. Harriet the Spy is the name of a book and a movie.

   _____

Lesson 2.15   Titles of Books and Movies

Proof It

Read the paragraphs below. Find the five book titles, and underline them.

Jon Scieszka (say **shez ka**) is a popular author. He has written many books for children. He is best known for his book The Stinky Cheese Man and Other Fairly Stupid Tales. Jon has always loved books. Dr. Seuss's famous book Green Eggs and Ham made Jon feel like he could be a writer one day.

In 1989, Jon wrote The True Story of the Three Little Pigs. Many children think his books are very funny. They also like the pictures. Lane Smith draws the pictures for many of Jon's books. They worked together on the book Math Curse. Their book Science Verse is also popular.

Try It

1. Write the title of your favorite book on the line below. Remember to underline it.

    _____

    _____

2. What was the last movie you saw? Write the title on the line below. Remember to underline it.

    _____

    _____

Review   Quotation Marks and Titles of Books and Movies

Quotation marks are used to show the exact words a person said. One set of quotation marks is used before the words. One set is used after the words.

> Zuri said, "My friend sent me a funny e-mail today."
>
> "Has the newspaper come yet?" asked Uncle Ned.

Book titles and movie titles are both underlined so the reader knows the words are part of a title.

> The librarian said I might like the book <u>Dragons Don't Cook Pizza</u>.
>
> Last night, my brother and I rented the movie <u>Finding Nemo</u>.

Putting It Together

Read the sentences below. Add quotation marks around the exact words a speaker says. Underline the titles of books and movies.

1. Ally, have you seen the movie Mary Poppins? asked Caroline.

2. The library has two copies of Cam Jansen and the Birthday Mystery.

3. Samina read the book Amber Brown Is Not a Crayon.

4. What time does Shark Tale start? Patrick asked.

5. Katsu said, I lent Daniel the book Caps for Sale.

6. Audrey asked, Would anyone like to watch the movie A Bug's Life?

Review ## Quotation Marks and Titles of Books and Movies

Read the paragraphs below. Look for the six book and movie titles. Underline each title.

Dr. Seuss's real name was Theodor Seuss Geisel. He may be one of the most loved children's authors. Dr. Seuss's first book was called And to Think That I Saw It on Mulberry Street. He wrote it in 1952. Children and adults love how silly his books are.

During his life, Dr. Seuss wrote 44 books for children. Did you ever read Green Eggs and Ham? Many children know this book by heart. Fox in Socks and Hop on Pop are two other books he wrote.

Some of Dr. Seuss's books have been made into movies. Jim Carrey starred in The Grinch. Mike Myers was in The Cat in the Hat.

Fill in the line in each sentence with your own answers. Remember to use quotation marks to show that someone is speaking. Also, remember to underline titles.

1. _____ is the funniest book I have ever read.

2. I think everyone should see the movie _____.

3. The movie _____ has a happy ending.

4. When she came from the dentist, Beatriz said, _____.

5. Steven looked at his watch and said, _____.

When there is only one person or thing, add **s** to the end of an action verb.

Caleb run**s** to the park.   Ms. Wheeler read**s** to us every day.

An action verb does not end with **s** when there is more than one person or thing, or when using **you**.

The balloons float through the air.   You pull the string.

Complete It

Read each sentence below. Then, read the pair of verbs in parentheses ( ). Choose the correct verb form. Write it on the line.

1. Wade _____ a game for the family. (pick, picks)

2. He _____ the wheel. (spin, spins)

3. Wade _____ a picture on a big sheet of paper. (draw, draws)

4. Mom and Dad _____. (laugh, laughs)

5. Alicia _____ what the picture is. (know, knows)

6. She _____ the bell. (ring, rings)

7. Alicia and Wade _____ a good team. (make, makes)

Lesson 3.1   Subject-Verb Agreement (Adding **s**)

Proof It

Read each sentence below. Add an **s** to the end of the verb if needed.

1. The Andersons love__ game night.

2. Alicia choose__ the game.

3. She pick__ her favorite board game.

4. Mom, Dad, Alicia, and Wade roll__ the dice.

5. Wade take__ the first turn.

6. He move__ his piece four spaces.

7. Mom roll__ the dice.

8. Uh-oh! Mom lose__ her turn.

9. Mom never win__ this game!

Try It

Use a pair of verbs from the box to write two sentences. One sentence should have only one person or thing. The other sentence should have more than one person or thing.

run, runs	play, plays
smile, smiles	throw, throws

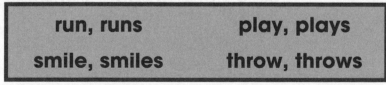

1. _____

2. _____

Lesson 3.2   # Subject-Verb Agreement (Adding **es**)

Sometimes, **es** needs to be added instead of just **s**. Add **es** to verbs that end in **sh**, **ch**, **s**, **x**, and **z**.

Ellie brush**es** her hair before she goes to bed.

Grandma stitch**es** the letters on the pillow.

He miss**es** his old house.

When there is more than one person or thing, verbs do not end in **s** or **es**.

Complete It

Read the sentences below. Choose the correct verb at the end of each sentence. Write it on the blank.

1. The bee _____ when it flies close to my ear. (buzz, buzzes)

2. Alexandra and Thomas _____ all the dishes after dinner. (wash, washes)

3. Manuel _____ the ball to Ashley. (toss, tosses)

4. Noelle _____ for something special when she blows out her candles. (wish, wishes)

5. Liam _____ the batter before he pours it in the pan. (mix, mixes)

Lesson 3.2 Subject-Verb Agreement (Adding **es**)

Solve It

Circle the verb in each sentence below. If it is correct, make a check mark (✓) on the line. If it is not correct, write the correct form. Then, see if you can find each verb in the word search puzzle. Circle the verbs you find in the puzzle. Words can be found across and down.

1. Mom and Dad relaxes on the weekends. _____

2. The snake hisses at the bird. _____

3. Liza catch the bus each morning. _____

4. Sean waxes his surfboard on the beach. _____

5. The red sports car pass the truck. _____

r	e	l	a	x	o	h	k
w	d	j	u	t	c	i	q
a	p	a	s	s	e	s	c
x	g	j	b	b	o	s	w
e	c	a	t	c	h	e	s
s	e	h	k	u	l	s	y

Try It

Write two sentences. Correctly use a verb from the box in each sentence.

touch	misses
fixes	push
rush	crashes

1. _____

_____

2. _____

_____

Lesson 3.3 Irregular Verbs: **Am**, **Is**, **Are**

Some verbs to do not show action. The verb **to be** does not show action. **Am**, **is**, and **are** are all different forms of the verb **to be**.

Am is used only with **I**.

I **am** happy.   I **am** behind the door.

Is is used when there is only one person or thing.

Tommy **is** my brother.   The sky **is** blue.

Are is used with you.

You **are** lucky.   You **are** my friend.

Are is also used when there is more than one person or thing.

Blanca and Charley **are** at school.   They **are** in second grade.

Complete It

Read each sentence below. Choose the correct verb from the parentheses ( ). Write it on the line.

1. I _____ tall and strong. (is, am)

2. You _____ a great cook. (are, am)

3. Gavin and Mitch _____ twins. (is, are)

4. This soup _____ too spicy! (is, am)

5. I _____ a niece. (are, am)

6. All the girls in my class _____ excited. (is, are)

7. That skateboard _____ broken. (are, is)

Lesson 3.3 Irregular Verbs: **Am**, **Is**, **Are**

Proof It

Read the diary entry below. The wrong forms of the verbs **am**, **is**, and **are** are used. Cross out each incorrect verb in bold type. Then, write the correct form above it.

Thursday, May 27

Dear Diary,

Victoria **are** my friend. She knows lots of jokes. Today, I told her, "You **am** the funniest person I know! I **are** glad to be your friend."

We **is** in a club together. Owen and Rachel **is** in the club, too. We learn all kinds of jokes. Knock-knock jokes **is** my favorite. Riddles **am** Victoria's favorite.

Owen **are** older than us. He **am** in third grade. He tells us all the third-grade jokes. We spend a lot of time laughing!

Try It

1. Write a sentence with only one person or thing. Use **is**.

_____

2. Write a sentence with more than one person or thing. Use **are**.

_____

Lesson 3.4 Irregular Verbs: **Has, Have**

Some verbs do not show action. The verb **to have** does not show action. **Has** and **have** are different forms of the verb **to have**.

Have is used with **I** or **you**.

I **have** six cats.   You **have** a bird.

Have is also used when there is more than one person or thing.

We **have** a French lesson this afternoon.

They **have** a green car.

Maureen and Ramon **have** brown hair.

The tree and the plant **have** leaves.

Has is used when there is only one person or thing.

She **has** two braids.   Lex **has** a book about fossils.

The moon **has** a rough surface.

Complete It

Read each sentence below. Then, read the pair of verbs in parentheses. Choose the correct verb form and write it on the line.

1. Maple trees and oak trees _____ similar leaves. (has, have)

2. A gingko tree _____ leaves that look like fans. (has, have)

3. We _____ a large fir tree in the backyard. (has, have)

4. The Maddens _____ many trees that bloom in the spring. (has, have)

5. Lila _____ an enormous, old maple tree in the front yard. (has, have)

Lesson 3.4 Irregular Verbs: **Has, Have**

Proof It

There is a mistake with the verb in each sentence below. Cross out the incorrect verb. Then, write the correct verb above it.

1. Holly trees has shiny red berries.

2. You has a beautiful weeping willow tree.

3. An apple tree have plenty of fruit in autumn.

4. A mulberry tree have berries that birds love to eat.

5. Jaya and Chad has a swing in the old oak tree.

6. I has a piece of bark from the white birch tree.

7. Sparrows and chickadees has a nest in the elm tree.

Try It

1. Write a sentence about something you have.

_____

_____

2. Write a sentence about something one of your friends has.

_____

_____

When there is only one person or thing in a sentence, the verb ends with **s**. When there is more than one person or thing, the verb does not end with **s**.

The cowboy put**s** on his hat.   The horses run across the field.

When there is only one person or thing, verbs that end in **sh**, **ch**, **s**, **x**, and **z** end in **es**.

The machine crush**es** the cans.

Aunt Fayza watch**es** the dancers.

Am, **is**, and **are** are different forms of the verb **to be**.
Am is used with **I**.

I **am** in the kitchen.   The wind **is** cold.

Are is used with **you** or when there is more than one person or thing

You **are** younger.   Bill and Ravi **are** first.

Has and **have** are different forms of the verb **to have**.
Have is used with **I** or **you**. **Have** is also used when there is more than one person or thing.

I **have** a sore throat.   You **have** blue eyes.

They **have** fun with their friends.

Noah and Ty **have** a trampoline.

Has is used when there is only one person or thing.

She **has** a sticker.   Quinn **has** a trumpet.

The bag **has** a handle.

Review ## Subject-Verb Agreement and Irregular Verbs

Putting It Together

Circle the verb in each sentence below. If it is correct, make a check mark (✓) in the space. If it is not correct, write the correct form in the space.

1. _____ The cricket hop across the field.

2. _____ Laurel catch a luna moth.

3. _____ The ant rushes toward the sticky candy wrapper.

4. _____ The ladybugs lands on the porch.

5. _____ The twins watches the praying mantis under the tree.

6. _____ The lightning bug flashes in the sky.

Read each sentence below. Then, read the pair of verbs in parentheses ( ). Choose the correct verb form, and write it in the space.

1. Zach and Grace _____ a butterfly garden. (have, has)

2. The grasshopper and the beetle _____ green. (is, are)

3. The inchworm _____ under the large rock. (am, is)

4. I _____ lucky that the dragonfly landed on my arm. (am, are)

5. The fly _____ two wings. (have, has)

Lesson 3.5   Forming the Past Tense by Adding **ed**

Verbs in the **present tense** tell about things that are happening right now. Verbs in the **past tense** tell about things that already happened. Add **ed** to most verbs to tell about the past.

Teresa jump**ed** over the log.   Grandma push**ed** the stroller.

The tall boy kick**ed** the ball.   Mr. Tisdall talk**ed** to the class.

If the verb already ends in **e**, just add **d**.

The family hik**ed** two miles. (hik**e**)

She plac**ed** the cups on the table. (plac**e**)

Complete It

The sentences below are missing verbs. Complete each sentence with the past tense of the verb in parentheses ( ).

1. Annie Smith Peck _____ to many countries. (travel)

2. In 1888, she _____ Mount Shasta in California. (climb)

3. She _____ to climb the Matterhorn one day. (hope)

4. Annie _____ a group called the American Alpine Club. (start)

5. She _____ the volcanoes of South America. (explore)

6. She _____ hard so she could climb in her spare time. (work)

7. Annie _____ climbing until she was 82. (continue)

Lesson 3.5   # Forming the Past Tense by Adding **ed**

Rewrite It

Rewrite the sentences below in the past tense by adding **ed** to the underlined verb. If the verb already ends in **e**, just add **d** to change it to the past tense.

Example: Darby <u>pull</u> on his leash.   Darby **pulled** on his leash.

1. Annie Smith Peck <u>climb</u> many mountains.

   _____

2. She <u>live</u> from 1850 until 1935.

   _____

3. Annie <u>show</u> the world how strong women can be.

   _____

4. She <u>want</u> to set records in climbing.

   _____

Try It

Write two sentences about what you did last week. Make sure the verbs are in the past tense.

1. _____

   _____

2. _____

   _____

Lesson 3.6 Past-Tense Verbs: **Was, Were**

The past tense of **am** and **is** is **was**. Remember to use was only if there is one person or thing.

I **was** tired.   The house **was** white.

The past tense of **are** is **were**. Remember to use **were** if there is more than one person or thing.

We **were** a team.   The monkeys **were** funny.

Complete It

Write the correct past-tense verb in the blanks below. Use **was** or **were**.

Last Tuesday, my brother Benjamin _____ on TV. He

_____ at the park with his friend Allison. It _____ a sunny

day. They _____ on the jungle gym. A news reporter _____

at the park, too. She _____ a reporter for Channel WBVA news.

She asked people in the park if the city

should build a new pool. Benjamin and

Allison _____ excited about the

interview. My family watched Benjamin

on the evening news. I _____ proud

of my brother, the TV star!

Lesson 3.6   Past-Tense Verbs: **Was, Were**

Rewrite It

The sentences below are in the present tense. Rewrite them in the past tense.

Example: The basketball is in the gym. The basketball was in the gym.

1. Benjamin is worried we would miss the news.

_____

_____

2. Mom and Dad are happy to see Ben's good manners.

_____

_____

3. I am glad Ben wore the hat I gave him.

_____

_____

4. You are on vacation.

_____

_____

Try It

1. Write a sentence about something that is happening right now. Use the verb **is** in your sentence.

_____

_____

2. Now, write the same sentence in the past tense.

_____

_____

Lesson 3.7 Past-Tense Verbs: **Had**

The past tense of **have** and **has** is **had**.

Present Tense
I **have** four pets.
The flowers **have** red petals.
Hayden **has** short hair.

Past Tense
I **had** four pets.
The flowers **had** red petals.
Hayden **had** short hair.

Complete It

Complete each sentence with the correct form of the verb **have**.
The word in parentheses ( ) will tell you to use the present tense or the
past tense.

1. My bike _____ a horn and a scoop seat. (present)

2. My mom _____ a bike just like it when she was little. (past)

3. The wheels _____ shiny silver spokes. (present)

4. My mom's old bike _____ a bell, too. (past)

Lesson 3.7 Past-Tense Verbs: **Had**

Identify It

Read each sentence below. Circle the verb. If the sentence is in the present tense, write **pres.** in the space. If it is in the past tense, write **past**.

1. _____ The one-dollar bill has a picture of George Washington on it.

2. _____ I had four dollars in my piggybank.

3. _____ The twenty-dollar bill has a picture of Andrew Jackson on it.

4. _____ Greg and Devi had ten dollars to spend at the bookstore.

5. _____ My sister has eight dollars.

6. _____ My parents have a can collection.

7. _____ Ian had a two-dollar bill.

Try It

1. Write a sentence about something you have.

_____

2. Now, rewrite your sentence in the past tense.

_____

Lesson 3.8   Past-Tense Verbs: **Went**

The past tense of the verb **go** is **went**.

<u>Present Tense</u>

We **go** to the fair with
   our cousins.
Lorenzo **goes** to Florida.

<u>Past Tense</u>

We **went** to the fair with our
   cousins.
Lorenzo **went** to Florida.

Rewrite It

Rewrite each sentence in the past tense.

1. We <u>go</u> to the store.

   _____

2. Trish <u>goes</u> to her singing lesson on Thursday.

   _____

3. Sanjay <u>goes</u> home at noon.

   _____

4. We <u>go</u> sledding with Miki and Ted.

   _____

Lesson 3.8   Past-Tense Verbs: **Went**

Proof It

Some of the verbs below are in the wrong tense. Cross out the underlined verbs. Write the correct past-tense verbs above them.

When my dad was little, his family <u>goes</u> to a cabin every summer. He loved the little cabin in the woods. His cousins came to visit. Everyone <u>goes</u> swimming in the lake. They <u>go</u> on long bike rides. They built forts in the woods. Grandma and Grandpa <u>go</u> for long walks. Once the entire family came from miles away. They <u>go</u> to a big family party on the beach.

Dad loved those summers in the woods. Some day, he will take us to see the old cabin.

Try It

1. Write a sentence using the verb **go** or **goes**.

_____

_____

2. Now, rewrite your sentence in the past tense.

_____

_____

Lesson 3.9   Past-Tense Verbs: **Saw**

The past tense of the verb **see** is **saw**.

Present Tense
My mom **sees** me swimming.
Franco and Ana **see** the
    puppy every day.

Past Tense
My mom **saw** me swimming.
Franco and Ana **saw** the
    puppy every day.

Rewrite It

Rewrite each sentence in the past tense.

1. We <u>see</u> raindrops on the leaves.

   _____

2. The dragon <u>sees</u> the little girl climbing the hill.

   _____

3. Dad <u>sees</u> the tiny cut when he put on his glasses.

   _____

4. The three birds <u>see</u> their mother.

   _____

5. Tess <u>sees</u> that movie three times.

   _____

6. Cameron and Dillon <u>see</u> the hot air balloon.

   _____

Lesson 3.9 Past-Tense Verbs: **Saw**

Proof It

Some of the verbs below are in the wrong tense. Cross out the underlined verbs. Write the correct past-tense verbs above them.

My aunt got married in Key West, Florida. We <u>see</u> many interesting things on our visit. My sister sees dolphins playing in the water. Dad took us to Ripley's Believe It or Not Museum. We <u>see</u> many strange and amazing things there. Later, we went to the Chicken Store. It is a place that rescues chickens. We <u>see</u> dozens of chickens there. I did not know Key West had so many homeless chickens!

Try It

1. What is the first thing you see when you wake up in the morning? Write your answer in the past tense.

_____

_____

2. What is the first thing you see when you go to school? Write your answer in the past tense.

_____

_____

Review # Regular and Irregular Past-Tense Verbs

Verbs in the **past tense** tell about things that already happened. To change most verbs to the past tense, add **ed**. If the verb already ends in **e**, just add **d**.

Grandpa toast**ed** the waffles.

The dogs race**d** across the field.

Some verbs do not follow the pattern of regular verbs. The past tenses of these verbs are different.

The past tense of **am** and **is** is **was**. The past tense of **are** is **were**.

Present Tense	Past Tense
I **am** thirsty.	I **was** thirsty.
The orange juice **is** cold.	The orange juice **was** cold.
Wes and Mary **are** seven.	Wes and Mary **were** seven.

The past tense of **has** and **have** is **had**.

Present Tense	Past Tense
The sisters **have** curly hair.	The sisters **had** curly hair.
The rabbit **has** silky fur.	The rabbit **had** silky fur.

The past tense of the verb **go** is **went**.

Present Tense	Past Tense
The geese **go** south.	The geese **went** south.
Tarek **goes** to the shop.	Tarek **went** to the shop.

The past tense of the verb **see** is **saw**.

Present Tense	Past Tense
I **see** six peppers in the bowl.	I **saw** six peppers in the bowl.

Review | # Regular and Irregular Past-Tense Verbs

Putting It Together

Complete each sentence below. Use the past tense of the verb in parentheses ( ).

1. Georgia O'Keeffe _____ a talented artist. (was, is)

2. She _____ flowers and desert scenes. (painted, paints)

3. She _____ two dogs named Bobo and Chia. (has, had)

4. Georgia _____ to New Mexico in the summers. (goes, went)

5. She _____ one of her favorite paintings Summer Days. (named, names)

The sentences below are in the present tense. Rewrite each sentence in the past tense.

1. Georgia O'Keeffe <u>sees</u> great beauty in the desert.

   _____

2. She <u>is</u> married to a photographer.

   _____

3. They <u>are</u> a very famous couple.

   _____

4. Georgia <u>lives</u> in a house called Rancho de los Burros.

   _____

Lesson 3.10 Contractions with **Not**

A **contraction** is a short way of saying something. In a contraction, two words are joined. An apostrophe (') goes in place of the missing letters.

Many contractions are formed with the word **not**. The apostrophe takes the place of the letter **o** in **not**.

is not = isn't	are not = aren't
was not = wasn't	were not = weren't
does not = doesn't	did not = didn't
have not = haven't	can not = can't

Match It

Match each pair of underlined words with its contraction. Write the letter of the contraction in the space.

1. _____ The cat and the mouse <u>are not</u> friends.   **a.** can't

2. _____ They <u>can not</u> get along.   **b.** isn't

3. _____ They <u>have not</u> tried very hard, though.   **c.** wasn't

4. _____ The cat <u>was not</u> friendly to the mouse.   **d.** weren't

5. _____ The mouse <u>is not</u> kind to the cat.   **e.** aren't

6. _____ I guess the cat and mouse <u>were not</u> meant   **f.** haven't
to live happily ever after.

Lesson 3.10 Contractions with **Not**

Rewrite It

Circle the two words in each sentence you
could combine to make a contraction. Then,
write the sentences using contractions.

1. Mr. Irving Mouse can not come out during the day.

   _____

2. He does not want to run into Miss Lola Cat.

   _____

3. Being chased is not Irving's idea of a good time.

   _____

4. He did not think Lola would be so rude.

   _____

5. They are not going to be able to share this house.

   _____

Try It

1. Write a sentence using one of the following pairs of words: **is not**,
   are not, **did not**, or **have not**

   _____

2. Now, rewrite your sentence using a contraction.

   _____

Lesson 3.11   Contractions with **Am**, **Is**, **Are**

Some contractions are formed with the words **am**, **is**, and **are**. The apostrophe takes the place of the letter **a** in **am**. It takes the place of **i** in **is**. It takes the place of **a** in **are**.

I am = I'm   you are = you're

we are = we're   they are = they're

it is = it's   he is = he's

she is = she's

Proof It

Read the diary entry below. Draw a line through the words in bold type. Then, write the contractions above the words.

Dear Diary,

    I am going to my karate class on Saturday morning. **It is** a class for beginners. Maria and Toby are taking karate, too. **They are** in my class. Maria learned some karate moves from her older brother. **He is** in a different class. Maria knows how to do more kicks than anyone else. I think **she is** the best student. Allan is our karate teacher. **He is** 39 years old. He has been doing karate since he was five. He has a black belt. Maria, Toby, and I plan to take lessons for a long time. **We are** going to get our black belts one day, too.

Lesson 3.11   # Contractions with **Am, Is, Are**

Complete It

Fill in the blanks below with a contraction from the box.

It's	You're	He's
We're	She's	They're

1. I think Allan is a great teacher. _____ patient and funny.

2. Maria's mom comes to every class. _____ interested in what we learn.

3. Toby and Maria are cousins. _____ both part of the Tarrano family.

4. Maria, Toby, and I will get our yellow belts next month. _____ excited to move up a level.

5. I like karate class a lot. _____ a good way to exercise and make friends.

6. Do you think you would like to try karate? _____ welcome to come watch one of our classes.

Try It

1. Write a sentence using the contraction for **she is**.

_____

2. Write a sentence using the contraction for **they are**.

_____

Lesson 3.12 Contractions with **Will**

Many contractions are formed with pronouns and the verb **will**. An apostrophe (') takes the place of the letters **wi** in **will**.

I will = I'll   it will = it'll
you will = you'll   we will = we'll
she will = she'll   they will = they'll
he will = he'll

Match It

Match each pair of underlined words with its contraction. Write the letter of the contraction in the space.

1. _____ <u>I will</u> travel into space one day.   **a.** She'll

2. _____ A spaceship will take me there. <u>It will</u> move very fast.   **b.** We'll

3. _____ <u>You will</u> be my co-pilot.   **c.** I'll

4. _____ My sister, Eva, can come along, too. <u>She will</u> direct the spaceship.   **d.** They'll

5. _____ <u>We will</u> make many important discoveries.   **e.** You'll

6. _____ Our families can have a party when we return. <u>They will</u> be so proud!   **f.** It'll

Lesson 3.12 ## Contractions with **Will**

Proof It

Read the newspaper article below. Draw a line through the underlined words. Then, write the contractions above the words.

Hughes to Become Youngest Astronaut

Jasmine Hughes is only nine years old. <u>She will</u> be the first child to journey into space. Jasmine has been training since she was four. <u>She will</u> travel on the space shuttle Investigator. Six other astronauts will be in her crew. <u>They will</u> have to work well as a team. Darren Unger will be the commander. <u>He will</u> be the leader of the crew. They know their mission is important. <u>It will</u> help scientists learn more about the universe. The world will be able to watch parts of the trip on TV. <u>We will</u> see history being made!

Try It

1. Write a sentence using the contraction for **he will**.

_____

_____

2. Write a sentence using the contraction for **I will**.

_____

_____

Review   Contractions

A **contraction** is a way to combine two words into one shorter word. An apostrophe (') goes in place of the missing letters.

Contractions can be formed with the word **not**. The apostrophe takes the place of the letter **o** in **not**.

is not = isn't   are not = aren't   have not = haven't

Contractions can be formed with the verbs **am**, **is**, and **are**. The apostrophe takes the place of the first letter in each verb.

I am = I'm   you are = you're   we are = we're

In contractions with **will**, an apostrophe takes the place of the letters **wi**.

she will = she'll   he will = he'll   it will = it'll

Putting It Together

Circle the two words in each sentence you could combine to make a contraction. Then, write the sentences using contractions.

1. Kumar and Meg have not painted a mural before.

_____

_____

2. They can not wait to begin.

_____

3. We will buy the paints and brushes tonight.

_____

Review Contractions

Match each pair of underlined words with its contraction. Write the letter of the contraction in the space.

1. _____ Kumar and Meg arrived at 8:00. They <u>were not</u> the first ones there.

    a. I'm

2. _____ Meg <u>did not</u> remember to bring an old shirt to wear.

    b. weren't

3. _____ <u>She is</u> going to borrow one from Mrs. Soh.

    c. She's

4. _____ <u>I am</u> going to paint a parrot, a banana tree, and two monkeys.

    d. didn't

5. _____ Our mural will show a rain forest. <u>It will</u> be beautiful.

    e. It'll

Read the following paragraph. Five contractions are misspelled. Draw a line through each incorrect contraction. Write the correct contraction above it.

    At first, Mrs. Soh was'nt sure that we should paint a rain forest. She did'nt know if the animals would be hard to paint. Kumar and I got some library books. The pictures werent' very big. But an artist came to the center to help us. He'is famous for painting murals all over town. He drew outlines of all the trees and animals. For his next project, hel'l paint an undersea scene on the side of a school.

Lesson 3.13   Plural Nouns with s

The word **plural** means **more than one**. To make most nouns plural, just add **s**.

one clock → two clock**s**   one shirt → three shirt**s**

one girl → many girl**s**   one squirrel → six squirrel**s**

Complete It

Read the sentences below. Complete each sentence with the plural form of the word in parentheses ( ).

Example: The _____boys_____ played tag until it got dark outside. (boy)

1. There are five blue _____ on Greece's flag. (stripe)

2. China's flag has five _____. (star)

3. The two _____ in Denmark's flag are red and white. (color)

4. Some flags have small _____ on them. (picture)

5. Jamaica's flag has four _____. (triangle)

6. _____ are on the flags of many countries. (Moon)

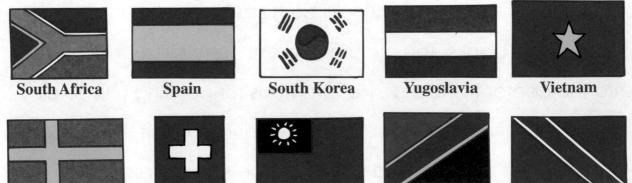

South Africa   Spain   South Korea   Yugoslavia   Vietnam

Sweden   Switzerland   Taiwan   Tanzania   Trinidad

Lesson 3.13   Plural Nouns with **s**

Solve It

The words below are all things that are on state flags of the United States. Write the plural form of each word on the line. Then, fill in the crossword puzzle using the numbers and the plural clues.

Down

1. date _____

2. bird _____

3. flower _____

5. tree _____

Across

4. animal _____

6. word _____

7. star _____

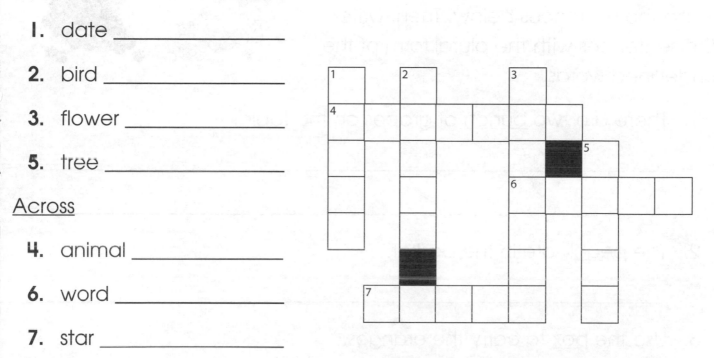

Try It

Write two sentences below. Use the plural form of at least one word from the box in each sentence.

paint	pencil	paintbrush
book	folder	pen
crayon	notebook	color

1. _____

2. _____

Lesson 3.14   Plural Nouns with **es**

If a noun ends in **sh**, **ch**, **s**, or **x**, add **es** to make it plural.

one ax → two ax**es**   one brush → many brush**es**

one pouch → six pouch**es**   one bus → seven bus**es**

Rewrite It

Read the sentences below. Then, write
the sentences with the plural form of the
underlined words.

1. There are two <u>bunch</u> of grapes on the table.

   _____

   _____

2. The <u>peach</u> are in the basket.

   _____

3. Use the <u>box</u> to carry the oranges.

   _____

4. Please put the fruit in the yellow <u>dish</u>.

   _____

   _____

5. Each of the <u>class</u> will get to pick some berries.

   _____

   _____

Lesson 3.14   Plural Nouns with **es**

Proof It

Read the paragraphs below. The underlined words should be plural. To make a word plural, make a caret (^) at the end of the word. Then, write the letter or letters you want to add above the caret.

Example: There are three **watch**^es in the glass case.

We waited on the <u>bench</u> outside the school. The <u>bus</u> picked us up at nine o'clock. We went to Sunnyvale Apple Orchard. Mr. Krup gave us some <u>box</u> to use. He showed us how to pick ripe apples. Many <u>branch</u> were heavy with fruit. There were also some blueberry <u>bush</u> on the farm.

When we were done picking, the tractor brought us back to the farmhouse. We ate our <u>lunch</u> at some picnic tables. Mrs. Krup gave us <u>glass</u> of lemonade. Tomorrow, we'll make apple pies.

Try It

Write two sentences below. Use the plural form of at least one word from the box in each sentence.

fox	watch
beach	brush

1. _____

2. _____

Lesson 3.15 Irregular Plural Nouns

Some plural nouns do not follow the rules you have learned. To form the plurals of these nouns, do not add **s** or **es**. Instead, the whole word changes. Here are some examples.

one **man** → three **men**   one **foot** → two **feet**

one **woman** → eight **women**   one **goose** → four **geese**

one **child** → a few **children**   one **tooth** → many **teeth**

one **mouse** → twenty **mice**

Some nouns do not change at all in their plural forms.

one **deer** → many **deer**   one **moose** → nine **moose**

one **fish** → sixty **fish**   one **sheep** → one hundred **sheep**

Match It

Read the phrases in Column 1. Then, draw a line to match each phrase to its plural in Column 2.

Column 1	Column 2
one tooth	nine deer
one child	four feet
one foot	twelve mice
one goose	several teeth
one deer	lots of children
one mouse	two men
one man	seven geese

Lesson 3.15 Irregular Plural Nouns

Solve It

Write the plural form of each word on the line.
Then, see if you can find each plural word in the
word search puzzle. Circle the words you find in the
puzzle. Words can be found across and down.

1. woman _____

2. fish _____

3. moose _____

4. mouse _____

5. foot _____

6. sheep _____

7. child _____

8. tooth _____

n	l	m	i	h	l	f	g	c	q
c	h	i	l	d	r	e	n	b	u
n	t	c	t	l	w	e	i	h	x
s	h	e	e	p	o	t	v	k	m
f	s	a	e	k	m	o	o	s	e
e	r	h	t	g	e	d	f	z	p
f	i	s	h	j	n	p	u	g	j

Try It

Write two sentences below. Use the
plural form of at least one word from
the box in each sentence.

foot	mouse
man	deer
fish	goose

1. _____

2. _____

Review # Regular and Irregular Plural Nouns

The word **plural** means **more than one**. To make most nouns plural, just add **s**.

boy → boy**s**   bug → bug**s**

If a noun ends in **sh**, **ch**, **s**, or **x**, add **es** to make it plural.

fox → fox**es**   wish → wish**es**

Some nouns do not follow the rules. Sometimes, the whole word changes in the plural. Sometimes, the word does not change at all.

man → **men**   mouse → **mice**   sheep → **sheep**

Putting It Together

All the underlined words should be plural. If a sentence is correct, make a check mark in the space (✓). If it is not correct, write the correct plural form on the line.

1. My <u>friend</u> and I went to the zoo. _____

2. We watched the <u>seals</u> play. _____

3. We saw hundreds of <u>fishes</u> at the aquarium. _____

4. We bought our <u>lunchs</u> at the Zoo Café. _____

5. I petted two shy <u>deers</u> at the petting zoo. _____

Review   Regular and Irregular Plural Nouns

Read each phrase below. Then, read the choices beside it. Choose the correct plural form. Write the letter on the line.

1. _____ one peach   a. two peaches   b. two peachs

2. _____ one dinosaur   a. fifty dinosaur   b. fifty dinosaurs

3. _____ one balloon   a. a few balloons   b. a few balloones

4. _____ one kiss   a. three kiss's   b. three kisses

5. _____ one goose   a. too many gooses   b. too many geese

6. _____ one sheep   a. six sheep   b. six sheeps

Read the paragraph below. On each line, write the plural form of the word in parentheses ( ).

The _____ (monkey) were playing on Monkey

Island. They swung from the _____ (branch) of two large

_____ (tree). They hid behind some _____

(bush). Finally, they waved their _____ (hand) and their

_____ (foot) at the crowd. A group of _____

(child) laughed at the funny _____ (animal). Two

_____ (man) who worked at the zoo said it was time to feed

the monkeys. They brought out some _____ (dish) filled with

_____ (treat). Then, the monkeys were too busy to play.

Lunchtime on Monkey Island is all about the food!

Lesson 3.16 Pronouns **I** and **Me**

I and **me** are both pronouns. **Pronouns** are words that take the places of nouns. The pronouns **I** and **me** are used when the writer is talking about himself or herself.

> **I** took the bus downtown. **I** bought a sandwich. The police officer waved to **me**. **I** walked to the museum. The woman behind the desk gave **me** a ticket.

When you are talking about yourself and another person, always put the other person first.

> **Robyn and I** left early.
> He gave the shells to **Dexter and me**.

Complete It

Complete each sentence below with the pronoun **I** or **me**. Write the pronoun in the space.

1. _____ was born in New York in 1899.

2. My five brothers and sisters were older than _____.

3. My wife and _____ moved to a farm in Maine.

4. _____ loved to read, write, and do chores on the farm.

5. A spider in my barn gave _____ the idea for a children's story.

Do you know who the mystery person is? It is E. B. White, the famous author of the books <u>Charlotte's Web</u> and <u>Stuart Little.</u>

Lesson 3.16　Pronouns **I** and **Me**

Proof It

Read the sentences below. If the correct pronoun is used, put a check mark on the line. If it is not, write the correct pronoun on the line.

1. _____ Me went to the store yesterday.

2. _____ Chris and I are on the same baseball team.

3. _____ Is that package for I?

4. _____ My sister and me are going to the playground.

5. _____ I had a great time last year at the museum.

6. _____ Running is good for I.

7. _____ Dad and me took the subway downtown.

8. _____ Amina gave I an invitation to the party.

Try It

On the lines below, write two sentences about things that happened to you last week. Use **I** in one sentence, and **me** in the other.

1. _____

_____

2. _____

_____

Lesson 3.17   Comparative Adjectives

Adjectives are words that describe nouns. They give the reader more information. Add **er** to an adjective to show that one thing is more than something else. Add **est** to an adjective to show that it is the most.

Rosa is tall.   Jill is tall**er**.   Bethany is tall**est**.

Identify It

Read the sentences below. Circle the correct adjective in parentheses.

1. Mount Everest is the (highest, higher) mountain.

2. The (tall, tallest) waterfall in the world is Angel Falls in Venezuela.

3. The Nile River is (longest, longer) than the Amazon River.

4. The Pacific Ocean is (deeper, deep) than the Indian Ocean.

5. It is the world's (deeper, deepest) ocean.

Lesson 3.17 Comparative Adjectives

Complete It

Fill in the spaces with the missing adjectives.

young	_____	youngest
_____	faster	fastest
dark	_____	_____
hard	harder	_____
new	_____	newest
_____	shorter	_____
small	_____	_____
kind	_____	kindest

Try It

On the lines below, write two sentences. Your sentences should compare people or things that are alike in some way.

Example: Stacey is older than Hasaan.   Val is the oldest.

1. _____

_____

2. _____

_____

Review   Pronouns **I** and **Me** and Comparative Adjectives

Use the pronouns **I** and **me** when you are talking about yourself.

    I made some pancakes on Mother's Day. My dad helped **me**.

    I brought my mom breakfast in bed. She smiled and gave **me** a big kiss.

Adjectives can be used to compare people or things. Add **er** to compare two things. Add **est** to compare more than two things.

    Tanner is young.   Mark is young**er**.   Cheng is the young**est**.

Putting It Together

Complete each sentence below with the pronoun **I** or **me**. Write the pronoun on the line.

1. Uncle Alex taught _____ about rocks and fossils.

2. Uncle Alex and _____ went to the Natural History Museum.

3. _____ have more than 50 rocks in my collection.

4. My uncle gave _____ a book about rocks for my birthday.

5. _____ can not wait to go on a rock-hunting trip with my uncle!

Review   Pronouns **I** and **Me** and Comparative Adjectives

Read each sentence below. Complete it with the correct form of the adjective in parentheses ( ).

Example: The blue jay is ____louder____ than the sparrow. (loud)

1. Diamonds are the _____ stone. (hard)

2. The gray rock is _____ than the black rock. (smooth)

3. The _____ rock in my collection has a fern fossil. (old)

4. The edges of the fossil are _____ than the other rocks. (rough)

5. My _____ rock is less than half an inch long. (small)

Read each sentence below. Then, write a new sentence on the line. Use a different form of the underlined adjective to compare.

Example: It is <u>cold</u> in autumn.   <u>It is colder in winter.</u>_____

1. The green book is <u>long</u>.

_____

2. The rug is <u>softer</u> than the floor.

_____

3. The orange juice is <u>sweet</u>.

_____

Review

Lesson 3.18   Synonyms

Synonyms are words that have the same, or almost the same, meanings. Synonyms can help you become a better writer. They make your writing more interesting to read. Here are some examples of synonyms.

little, tiny, small   easy, simple

begin, start   quick, fast

under, below   laugh, giggle

Match It

Match each word in the first column with its synonym in the second column. Write the letter of the synonym on the line.

I. _____ beautiful		**a.** enjoy
2. _____ boat		**b.** toss
3. _____ like		**c.** happy
4. _____ tired		**d.** ship
5. _____ grin		**e.** pal
6. _____ glad		**f.** sleepy
7. _____ friend		**g.** pretty
8. _____ throw		**h.** smile

Lesson 3.18 Synonyms

Complete It

Read the sentences below. Each underlined word has a synonym in the box. Write the synonym on the line at the end of the sentence.

giggled	bugs	hop
dad	pick	liked	terrific

1. Malik needed to <u>choose</u> a topic for his report. _____

2. He and his <u>father</u> sat down at the computer. _____

3. Malik <u>enjoyed</u> using the Internet for school projects. _____

4. All of a sudden, he had a <u>great</u> idea. _____

5. "I think I'm going to do my report on <u>insects</u>," Malik told his dad. _____

6. Malik and Dad watched a cartoon cricket <u>jump</u> across the computer screen. _____

7. Malik <u>laughed</u> when the cricket stopped and waved. _____

Try It

1. Write a sentence using a synonym for the word **small**.

_____

2. Write a sentence using a synonym for the word **yelled**.

_____

Lesson 3.19 Antonyms

An **antonym** is a word that means the opposite of another word. Here are some examples of antonyms.

big, little	old, young
happy, sad	first, last
right, wrong	never, always

Identify It

There are two antonyms in each sentence below. Circle each pair of antonyms.

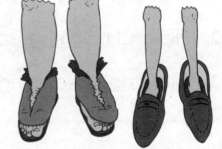

1. The tall bottle is next to the short can.

2. Kent wore his new shirt with his favorite pair of old jeans.

3. I thought the quiz would be hard, but it was easy.

4. Did Miranda smile or frown when she saw you?

5. One pair of shoes is too tight, and one pair is too loose.

6. Open the cupboard, take out the cereal, and close the door.

7. It was hot outside, but it will be cold tomorrow.

8. Stephen was the first person in line and the last person to leave.

9. Would you rather go in the morning or night?

Lesson 3.19 Antonyms

Solve It

In the spaces, write an antonym for each word below. Then, circle the antonyms in the word search puzzle. Words can be found across and down.

1. yell __ __ __ __ __ __ __

2. pull __ __ __ __

3. empty __ __ __ __

4. win __ __ __ __

5. yes __ __

6. love __ __ __ __

7. over __ __ __ __ __

8. down __ __

q	a	w	h	i	s	p	e	r	p
f	u	l	l	c	g	u	p	j	t
m	n	n	o	k	h	s	p	x	a
a	d	g	s	y	b	h	a	t	e
z	e	b	e	o	l	p	f	d	j
d	r	l	c	h	z	k	p	l	o

Try It

1. Write a sentence using an antonym for **loud**.

_____

2. Write a sentence using an antonym for **soft**.

_____

Review Synonyms and Antonyms

Synonyms are words that have the same, or almost the same, meanings.

throw, toss   close, near

quick, fast   sad, unhappy

huge, giant   beautiful, pretty

Antonyms are words that mean the opposite of one another.

up, down   happy, sad

heavy, light   hot, cold

new, old   smooth, rough

Putting It Together

Read each pair of sentences. If the underlined words are synonyms, write **S** in the blank. If they are antonyms, write **A** in the blank.

1. _____ Colby's puppet had <u>dark</u> hair.
   Nina's puppet had <u>light</u> hair.

2. _____ <u>First</u>, Colby painted a face on his puppet.
   The <u>last</u> thing Nina did was button her puppet's dress.

3. _____ Nina tied a <u>little</u> bow in her puppet's hair.
   Colby's puppet had a <u>small</u> frog in its pocket.

4. _____ "You did a <u>great</u> job painting your puppet's face," said Nina.
   "I think your puppet is <u>terrific</u>," said Colby.

Review   # Synonyms and Antonyms

There is an antonym in the box for each underlined word. Write the antonyms above them.

below	same	few
huge	small	hard
sits	boring	outside

There are many <u>different</u> kinds of puppets. Some are <u>tiny</u>. They are called finger puppets. Others are quite <u>large</u>. Hand puppets are <u>easy</u> to use. You just put one hand <u>inside</u> the puppet. Then, you can move the puppet's head and arms.

String puppets are harder to use. The person <u>stands</u> <u>above</u> the puppet and moves the strings. There might be as <u>many</u> as 30 strings! Watching a puppet show can be very <u>exciting</u>.

Read the sentences below. If there is an **A** after the sentence, write an antonym for the underlined word. If there is an **S**, write a synonym.

1. Children all around the world have <u>hated</u> Jim Henson's Muppets.

   A _____

2. When he was <u>old</u>, Jim made a puppet from his mother's old coat.

   A _____

3. On *Sesame Street*, Bert and Ernie are good <u>friends</u>.

   S _____

Lesson 3.20 Homophones

Homophones are words that sound alike but have different spellings and meanings. Here are some examples of homophones.

to = toward   We went **to** the gym.
OR
use **to** with a verb   Dennis wants **to** skate.
two = the number that   Give the dog **two** biscuits.
   comes after one

too = also   We will go, **too**.
OR
too = very; more than enough   Lindy is **too** young to go.

by = next to   The bag is **by** the door.
bye = good-bye   Karim waved and said **bye**.
buy = to purchase something   I will **buy** three pears.

right = the opposite of wrong   That is the **right** answer.
write = to record your words   **Write** a report about the book.

Complete It

Choose the correct word to complete each sentence. Write it on the line.

1. I would like _____ see *Pinocchio* on ice. (to, too)

2. My sister wants to go, _____. (two, too)

3. Mom said she will try to _____ tickets tonight. (bye, buy)

4. I am going to _____ about the show in my diary. (write, right)

Lesson 3.20 Homophones

Proof It

Read the poster below. There are five mistakes. Cross out each mistake. Then, write the correct homophone above it.

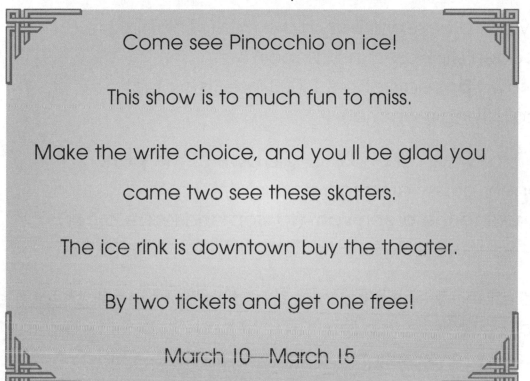

Come see Pinocchio on ice!

This show is to much fun to miss.

Make the write choice, and you ll be glad you came two see these skaters.

The ice rink is downtown buy the theater.

By two tickets and get one free!

March 10—March 15

Try It

1. Write a sentence using the word **too**.

   _____

2. Write a sentence using the word **buy**.

   _____

3. Write a sentence using the word **write**.

   _____

Lesson 3.21 Multiple-Meaning Words

Multiple-meaning words are words that are spelled the same but have different meanings. You have to read the sentence carefully to know which meaning a writer wants to use.

Casey got a baseball **bat** and a mitt for his birthday.
(a wooden stick used in baseball)
The brown **bat** eats about 2,000 insects a night.
(a small, flying mammal)

There is a swing set and a jungle gym at the **park**.
(an open, grassy area for relaxing)
Park next to the green van. (to stop and leave a car)

Find It

Read this dictionary entry. It shows two different meanings for the same word. Each meaning is a different part of speech. Use the dictionary entry to answer the questions below.

cold *adj.* having a low temperature; cool, chilly, or icy; not warm; *noun* an illness that often includes a cough, a sore throat, and a runny nose

1. It will be cold but sunny on Saturday.

   Which definition of **cold** is used in this sentence? _____
   a. the first definition   **b.** the second definition

2. Destiny caught a cold from her brother.
   Which definition of **cold** is used in this sentence? _____
   a. the first definition   **b.** the second definition

Lesson 3.21   Multiple-Meaning Words

Match It

Look at the definitions of the underlined word. Choose the definition that matches the way the word is used. Write the letter of that definition on the line.

1. _____ Airplanes <u>fly</u> at amazing speeds.
   a. a small insect with two wings
   b. to move through the air

2. _____ The <u>leaves</u> were red, gold, and brown.
   a. parts of a tree or a plant   **b.** goes away

3. _____ May I <u>pet</u> your cat?
   a. an animal that lives with people
   b. to touch lightly or stroke

4. _____ The Krugers did not <u>watch</u> the entire movie.
   a. view or look at   **b.** a small clock worn on the wrist

5. _____ Keely will <u>train</u> her puppy to roll over.
   a. to teach something by doing it over and over
   b. a long line of cars that run on a track

Try It

The word **fair** can have two meanings: **equal** or **a place, like a carnival, where there are rides and games.** Write two sentences using the word **fair**. It should have a different meaning in each sentence.

1. _____

2. _____

Review   # Homophones and Multiple-Meaning Words

Homophones are words that sound the same but have different spellings and meanings.

To, **too**, and **two** are homophones.

Susan walked her **two** dogs.   Can I come, **too**?

Keith forgot **to** put away the milk.

By, **buy**, and **bye** are homophones.

Lane sat **by** Kofi.   I will **buy** a muffin.

He said **bye** and quickly left.

Right and **write** are homophones.

Don't forget to **write** to me!

"You are **right**!" said Ms. Greene.

Multiple-meaning words are words that are spelled the same but have different meanings. You have to read the sentence carefully to know which meaning a writer wants to use.

The **leaves** are starting to change already. (the parts of a tree that change color)

Mr. Fromm **leaves** at 7:00 in the morning. (goes away)

Putting It Together

Read the paragraph below. Circle the correct homophone from the pair in parentheses ( ).

When I leave for school, I say (buy, bye) to my little sister. She wishes she could go (to, two) school, (two, too), but she is not old enough. We are going to make a pretend school for her at home. My parents said they will (by, buy) us a chalkboard. We will put it (by, bye) the desk and the (too, two) small chairs. I will teach Melissa how to (write, right). She already knows the (write, right) way to make all the letters. She can't wait for school (to, too) start!

Review Homophones and Multiple-Meaning Words

Use the dictionary entry to answer the questions below.

saw *verb* the past tense of the verb **see**
      noun a sharp tool used for cutting

1. The old woodcutter used a saw to cut the firewood. Which definition of **saw** is used in this sentence? _____
   a. the first definition   **b.** the second definition

2. Jonah saw his favorite movie 16 times! Which definition of **saw** is used in this sentence? _____
   a. the first definition   **b.** the second definition

1. Write a sentence using the word **two**.

   _____

2. Write a sentence using the word **by**.

   _____

3. Write a sentence using the word **watch**. In your sentence, **watch** should **mean a small clock worn on the wrist**.

   _____

4. Write a sentence using the word **pet**. In your sentence, **pet** should mean **an animal that lives with people**.

   _____

NAME _____

Writer's Guide: Planning

Before you start writing, you need to make a plan. **Brainstorming** is one way to come up with ideas. You may not use all of your ideas. Still, you will find the one or two great ideas you were looking for.

Sit down with a pen and a piece of paper. Make a list of things you know a lot about or would like to learn more about.

life in the Sahara desert	Eiffel Tower
basketball	space shuttles
islands	being an artist

Which topic is most interesting? Once you choose your topic, you can start learning more about it. You may need to go to the library. You may need to use the Internet. You may even need to interview someone.

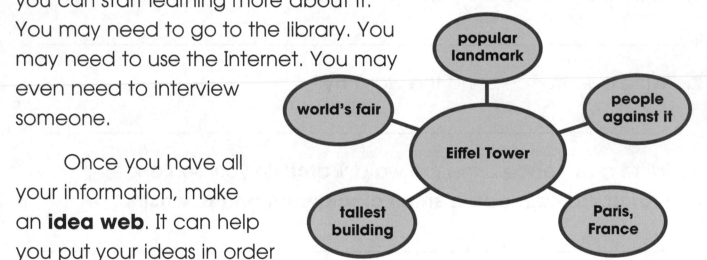

Once you have all your information, make an **idea web**. It can help you put your ideas in order before you start writing.

Try It

On a separate piece of paper, brainstorm your own list of ideas. Let your imagination go, and have fun! Choose the most interesting topic. If you need to, look for more information. Then, create an idea web.

Lesson 4.2   Writer's Guide: Writing

When you first begin writing, do not worry about mistakes. You are just writing a **rough draft**. Look at the idea web you made when you were planning. Turn your ideas into sentences and paragraphs.

Do not worry about editing right now. After you have written your first draft, you can make changes and corrections. For now, just write. Here are some things to keep in mind as you write:

- Stay on topic.
- Include all the important details.
- Use complete sentences.

Here is an example of a rough draft. Can you see how the writer used the idea web to help write this paragraph?

The Eiffel Tower is an intresting place to visit. It was built in Paris France. It was made for a world's fair The Louvre is a famous museum in Paris. The tower is very tall. It was the tallest building in the world many people did not think it should be built. it looks like they were wrong, though. Millions of people visit it every year! It is one of the most famus landmarks.

Try It

Use the idea web you made to write a rough draft on another piece of paper. Remember, this stage is all about writing, so write! You'll be able to edit your work later.

Lesson 4.3   Writer's Guide: Revising

Now that you have finished writing, it is time to **revise**. Read what you have written. Sometimes it helps to read your work out loud. Ask yourself these questions:

- Do all of my sentences tell about the main idea?
- Can I add any details that make my writing more interesting?
- Are there any words or sentences that do not belong?

The Eiffel tower is an intresting place to visit. It was built ^in ^in 1889

Paris France. It was made for a world's fair. ~~The Louvre is a famous~~
986 feet
~~museum in Paris.~~ The tower is ^very tall. It was the tallest building in
for 41 years   They thought it would be ugly.
the world ^many people did not think it should be built. ^it looks like
About 6   ↗   The Eiffel tower
they were wrong, though. ^Millions ~~of~~ people visit ~~it~~ ^every year! It is
in the world
one of the most famus landmarks. ^

In the paragraph above, the writer added some details. For example, explaining that the Eiffel Tower is very tall does not tell the reader much. It is more helpful to know that the Eiffel Tower is 986 feet tall.

The writer also took out a sentence that was not needed. The Louvre is in Paris, but it does not have anything to do with the Eiffel Tower. The writer decided that the sentence about the Louvre was not on topic.

Try It

Look at all the changes the writer made. Can you see why each change was needed? Now, revise your rough draft. Doesn't it sound better already?

Lesson 4.4   # Writer's Guide: Proofreading

Proofreading makes your writing stronger and clearer. Here are some things to ask yourself when you are proofreading:

- Do sentences and proper nouns start with a capital letter?
- Does each sentence end with a punctuation mark?
- Are any words misspelled? Use a dictionary if you are not sure.
- Are commas used in the right places?

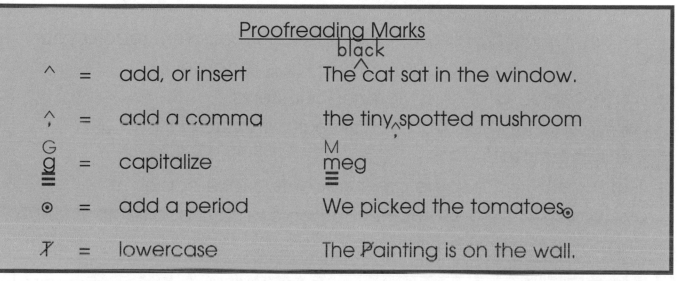

Proofreading Marks

∧	=	add, or insert	The cat sat in the window. (black)
⌄	=	add a comma	the tiny spotted mushroom
g	=	capitalize	meg (M)
⊙	=	add a period	We picked the tomatoes⊙
⁄	=	lowercase	The Painting is on the wall.

The Eiffel Tower is an intresting place to visit. It was built in 1889 in Paris France. It was made for a world's fair. The tower is 986 feet tall. It was the tallest building in the world for 41 years many people did not think it should be built. They thought it would be ugly. it looks like they were wrong, though. About six Million people visit the Eiffel tower every year! It is one of the most famus landmarks in the world.

Try It

Use proofreading marks to edit your writing. Trade papers with a friend. It can be easier to spot mistakes in someone else's work.

Lesson 4.5   Writer's Guide: Publishing

After all your changes have been made, write or type a final copy of your work. Your paper should look neat and clean. Now, you are ready to publish. **Publishing** is a way of sharing your writing with others. Here are some ways to publish your work:

- Read your writing to your family, your friends, or your classmates.
- Make a copy of your writing. Send it to someone who lives far away.
- Read your writing aloud. Have a teacher or parent record you. You can use a video camera or a tape recorder.
- Make copies, and give them to your friends.
- Ask an adult to help you e-mail your writing to a friend or a family member.
- Get together with some other students. Make copies of everyone's writing. Combine the copies into a booklet that each student can take home.

From: Tucker Boone
Date: May 20, 2015
To: auntlouisa@smileyhorse.net; grandpajoe@21stcentury.com
Subject: Eiffel Tower report

The Eiffel Tower is an interesting place to visit. It was built in 1889 in Paris, France. It was made for a world's fair. The tower is 986 feet tall. It was the tallest building in the world for 41 years. Many people did not think it should be built. They thought it would be ugly. It looks like they were wrong, though. About six million people visit the Eiffel Tower every year! It is one of the most famous landmarks in the world.

Try It

Choose one of the ways listed above to share your work. What kinds of comments do your friends and family have? Can you think of any other ways to share your writing?

Lesson 4.6   Writer's Guide: Writing a Paragraph

LA TOUR EIFFEL

A **paragraph** is a group of sentences. Each paragraph is about one main idea. All the sentences tell more about the main idea. When you are ready to write about a new idea, start a new paragraph. When the paragraphs are put together, they make a letter, a story, or a report.

A new paragraph does not start at the left edge of a piece of paper. It starts about five spaces from the edge. Leave an **indent**, or a space, about the size of the word **write**. This space tells the reader a new paragraph is starting.

The first sentence in a paragraph is the **topic sentence**. It tells what the paragraph will be mostly about. The next few sentences give more details about the topic. The last sentence is a **closing sentence**. It sums up the paragraph.

In the paragraph below, each important part is labeled.

indent   **topic sentence**

details

→ <u>The Eiffel Tower is an interesting place to visit.</u> It was built in 1889 in Paris, France. It was made for a world's fair. The tower is 986 feet tall. It was the tallest building in the world for 41 years. Many people did not think it should be built. They thought it would be ugly. It looks like they were wrong, though. About six million people visit the Eiffel Tower every year! <u>It is one of the most famous landmarks in the world.</u>

closing sentence

Lesson 4.7 Writer's Guide: Writing a Friendly Letter

Writing a letter can be fun. It is exciting to open the mailbox and see a letter waiting. Writing letters can also be a good way to keep in touch with people who live far away.

Here are some things to keep in mind when you write a letter:

- **Write the date in the top right corner.** Remember to start the name of the month with a capital letter. Use a comma between the day and the year.
- **Begin your letter with a greeting.** Follow it with the person's name and a comma. Most letters begin with the word Dear.
- **Share some news in your letter.** What is new in your life? Have you done anything fun? Have you been someplace exciting?
- **Ask questions.** It is polite to ask how others are doing.
- **End your letter with a closing.** Some popular closings are **Sincerely**, **Yours truly**, **Love**, and **Your friend**. Use a capital letter to begin your closing. Use a comma after it.
- **Sign your name** below the closing.

May 20, 2014

Dear Grandma,

How are you? I am doing fine. Last week, I wrote a report about the Eiffel Tower. Mom helped me do some research on the Internet. I learned many interesting facts. For example, did you know that the Eiffel Tower has 1,665 steps? Mr. Strasser said my report was excellent. I told him that I plan to see the Eiffel Tower in person someday.

Please write back to me, and tell me what's new in Park City. I miss you a lot and hope you can visit soon.

Love,
Tucker

Lesson 4.8   Writer's Guide: Writing to Convince

Have you ever tried to convince someone of something? To **convince** means **to get people to see things your way**. Maybe you have tried to convince your teacher that recess should be longer. Maybe you have tried to convince your parents to give you a later bedtime.

Words can be very powerful. You can change people's ideas with your words. Here are some tips for writing to convince:

* Think of all the reasons you feel a certain way. Make a list of your ideas.
* Now, think about why people might not agree with you. What could you say to change their minds? Add these ideas to your list.
* You are ready to begin writing. First, write a topic sentence about what you want or believe. Next, list your reasons. Finally, write a sentence that sums up your ideas.

Eiffel Tower should be free	it's a public place
	more people might visit if free
	people could donate money
	money used to care for tower

People should not have to pay to visit the Eiffel Tower. The tower is like a park or a library. It belongs to everyone. People should be able to enjoy it at any time. Instead of paying to see it, people could donate money if they wanted. This money could be used to take care of the tower. More people might visit the Eiffel Tower if they did not have to pay. It should be free for everyone to enjoy.

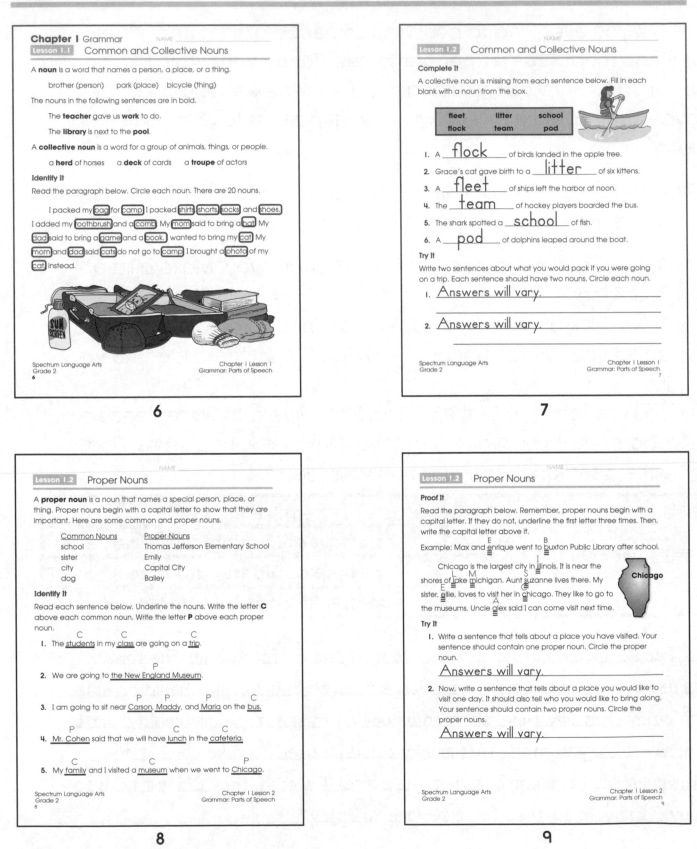

Chapter 1 Grammar   NAME _____
Lesson 1.1   Common and Collective Nouns

A **noun** is a word that names a person, a place, or a thing.

    brother (person)   park (place)   bicycle (thing)

The nouns in the following sentences are in bold.

    The **teacher** gave us **work** to do.

    The **library** is next to the **pool**.

A **collective noun** is a word for a group of animals, things, or people.

    a **herd** of horses   a **deck** of cards   a **troupe** of actors

Identify It

Read the paragraph below. Circle each noun. There are 20 nouns.

I packed my (bag) for (camp). I packed (shirts), (shorts), (socks), and (shoes). I added my (toothbrush) and a (comb). My (mom) said to bring a (hat). My (dad) said to bring a (game) and a (book). I wanted to bring my (cat). My (mom) and (dad) said (cats) do not go to (camp). I brought a (photo) of my (cat) instead.

Chapter 1 Lesson 1
Grammar: Parts of Speech

6

Lesson 1.2   Common and Collective Nouns

Complete It

A collective noun is missing from each sentence below. Fill in each blank with a noun from the box.

| fleet | litter | school |
| flock | team | pod |

1. A __flock__ of birds landed in the apple tree.
2. Grace's cat gave birth to a __litter__ of six kittens.
3. A __fleet__ of ships left the harbor at noon.
4. The __team__ of hockey players boarded the bus.
5. The shark spotted a __school__ of fish.
6. A __pod__ of dolphins leaped around the boat.

Try It

Write two sentences about what you would pack if you were going on a trip. Each sentence should have two nouns. Circle each noun.

1. __Answers will vary.__

2. __Answers will vary.__

Chapter 1 Lesson 1
Grammar: Parts of Speech
7

7

Lesson 1.2   Proper Nouns

A **proper noun** is a noun that names a special person, place, or thing. Proper nouns begin with a capital letter to show that they are important. Here are some common and proper nouns.

Common Nouns	Proper Nouns
school	Thomas Jefferson Elementary School
sister	Emily
city	Capital City
dog	Bailey

Identify It

Read each sentence below. Underline the nouns. Write the letter **C** above each common noun. Write the letter **P** above each proper noun.

1. The <u>students</u> (C) in my <u>class</u> (C) are going on a <u>trip</u> (C).

2. We are going to <u>the New England Museum</u> (P).

3. I am going to sit near <u>Carson</u> (P), <u>Maddy</u> (P), and <u>Maria</u> (P) on the <u>bus</u> (C).

4. <u>Mr. Cohen</u> (P) said that we will have <u>lunch</u> (C) in the <u>cafeteria</u> (C).

5. My <u>family</u> (C) and I visited a <u>museum</u> (C) when we went to <u>Chicago</u> (P).

Chapter 1 Lesson 2
Grammar: Parts of Speech

8

Lesson 1.2   Proper Nouns

Proof It

Read the paragraph below. Remember, proper nouns begin with a capital letter. If they do not, underline the first letter three times. Then, write the capital letter above it.

Example: Max and <u>e</u>nrique went to <u>b</u>uxton Public Library after school.

Chicago is the largest city in <u>i</u>llinois. It is near the shores of <u>l</u>ake <u>m</u>ichigan. Aunt <u>s</u>uzanne lives there. My sister, <u>e</u>llie, loves to visit her in <u>c</u>hicago. They like to go to the museums. Uncle <u>a</u>lex said I can come visit next time.

Try It

1. Write a sentence that tells about a place you have visited. Your sentence should contain one proper noun. Circle the proper noun.

    __Answers will vary.__

2. Now, write a sentence that tells about a place you would like to visit one day. It should also tell who you would like to bring along. Your sentence should contain two proper nouns. Circle the proper nouns.

    __Answers will vary.__

Chapter 1 Lesson 2
Grammar: Parts of Speech
9

9

Answer Key

Lesson 1.3 Pronouns

A **pronoun** is a word that takes the place of a noun. Some pronouns are **I, me, you, he, she, him, her, it, we, us, they,** and **them.**

In the sentences below, pronouns take the place of the underlined nouns.

Drew and Lei play softball every Saturday.
They play softball every Saturday.

Dad parked the car in the garage.
Dad parked **it** in the garage.

Reflexive pronouns end in **self** or **selves.**
Myself, yourself, himself, herself, itself, ourselves, and **themselves** are reflexive pronouns.

Identify It

Circle the pronouns in the following paragraph. There are 12 pronouns.

(I) will never forget the first soccer game (I) ever saw. Mom, Dad, Laura, and (I) drove downtown to the stadium. (It) was lit up against the night sky. (We) were excited to see the Rangers play. The stadium was filled with hundreds of people. (They) cheered when the players ran onto the field. Laura and (I) screamed and clapped (ourselves) silly. (We) laughed when the Rangers' mascot did a funny dance. The best part of the game was when Matt Ramos scored the winning goal. (He) is the best player on the team. (It) was a night to remember for (myself) and my family!

Spectrum Language Arts
Grade 2
10

Chapter 1 Lesson 3
Grammar: Parts of Speech

10

Lesson 1.3 Pronouns

Complete It

Read each pair of sentences below. Choose the correct pronoun from the pair in parentheses ( ) to take the place of the underlined word or words. Write it in the space.

1. Mom drove Anna to soccer practice. Mom drove ___her___ (you, her) to soccer practice.

2. Dan and Marco are on Anna's team. ___They___ (Him, They) are on Anna's team.

3. Anna kicked the ball out of bounds. ___She___ (She, Her) kicked the ball out of bounds.

4. The coach talked to the players. The coach talked to ___them___ (she, them).

Rewrite It

Fill in each blank below with a reflexive pronoun.

1. The team served ___themselves___ a snack after the game.

2. Anna cut ___herself___ when she tripped over a rock.

3. Tim blamed ___himself___ for not checking the field better.

4. "You should be proud of ___yourselves___ for a great game!" said Coach.

Spectrum Language Arts
Grade 2

Chapter 1 Lesson 3
Grammar: Parts of Speech
11

11

Lesson 1.4 Verbs

Verbs are an important part of speech. They are often action words. They tell what happens in a sentence. The verbs in the sentences below are in bold.

Sadie **raced** down the stairs. She **barked** at the cat on the windowsill. Then, she **wagged** her tail at Mrs. Callahan. Sadie **ate** the treat from Mrs. Callahan's hand.

Solve It

Find the verb in each sentence. Write it in the spaces under the sentence.

1. Akiko placed her new puppy on the rug in the living room.

pl(a)ced

2. The puppy sniffed the rug and the couch.

s(n)iffed

3. The puppy ran in circles around the room.

ra(n)

4. Akiko and her dad giggled at the excited little dog.

g(i)ggled

5. The puppy chewed on Akiko's green slipper.

chew(e)d

What is Akiko's puppy's name? Write the circled letters from your answers on the lines below to spell out the puppy's name.

Annie

Spectrum Language Arts
Grade 2
12

Chapter 1 Lesson 4
Grammar: Parts of Speech

12

Lesson 1.4 Verbs

Complete It

Fill in each blank with a verb from the box. Some verbs can be used in more than one sentence.

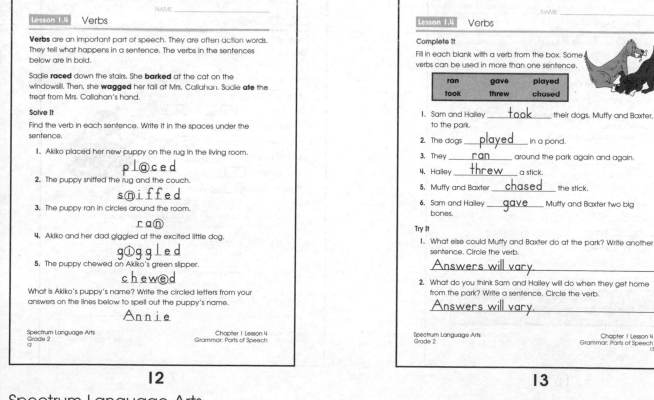

ran	gave	played
took	threw	chased

1. Sam and Hailey ___took___ their dogs, Muffy and Baxter, to the park.

2. The dogs ___played___ in a pond.

3. They ___ran___ around the park again and again.

4. Hailey ___threw___ a stick.

5. Muffy and Baxter ___chased___ the stick.

6. Sam and Hailey ___gave___ Muffy and Baxter two big bones.

Try It

1. What else could Muffy and Baxter do at the park? Write another sentence. Circle the verb.

Answers will vary.

2. What do you think Sam and Hailey will do when they get home from the park? Write a sentence. Circle the verb.

Answers will vary.

Spectrum Language Arts
Grade 2

Chapter 1 Lesson 4
Grammar: Parts of Speech
13

13

Spectrum Language Arts
Grade 2

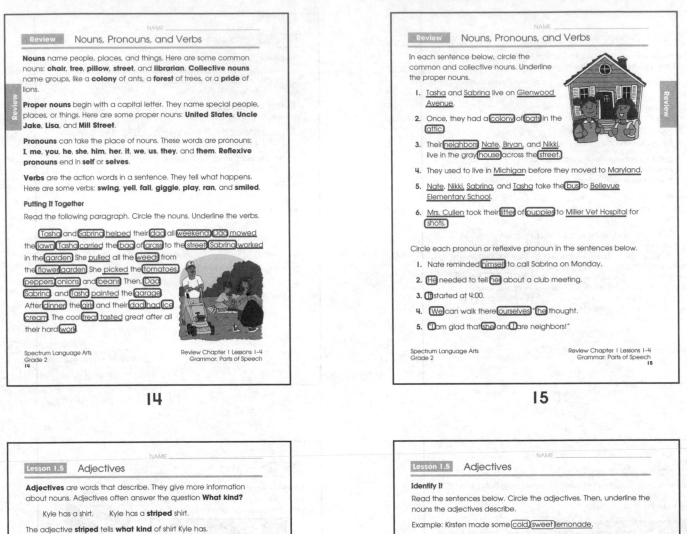

Review | Nouns, Pronouns, and Verbs

Nouns name people, places, and things. Here are some common nouns: **chair, tree, pillow, street,** and **librarian. Collective nouns** name groups, like a **colony** of ants, a **forest** of trees, or a **pride** of lions.

Proper nouns begin with a capital letter. They name special people, places, or things. Here are some proper nouns: **United States, Uncle Jake, Lisa,** and **Mill Street.**

Pronouns can take the place of nouns. These words are pronouns: **I, me, you, he, she, him, her, it, we, us, they,** and **them. Reflexive pronouns** end in **self** or **selves.**

Verbs are the action words in a sentence. They tell what happens. Here are some verbs: **swing, yell, fall, giggle, play, ran,** and **smiled.**

Putting It Together

Read the following paragraph. Circle the nouns. Underline the verbs.

Tasha and Sabrina helped their dad all weekend. Dad mowed the lawn. Tasha carried the bag of grass to the street. Sabrina worked in the garden. She pulled all the weeds from the flower garden. She picked the tomatoes, peppers, onions, and beans. Then, Dad, Sabrina, and Tasha painted the garage. After dinner, the girls and their dad had ice cream. The cool treat tasted great after all their hard work.

Spectrum Language Arts
Grade 2
14

Review Chapter 1 Lessons 1–4
Grammar: Parts of Speech

14

Review | Nouns, Pronouns, and Verbs

In each sentence below, circle the common and collective nouns. Underline the proper nouns.

1. Tasha and Sabrina live on Glenwood Avenue.
2. Once, they had a colony of bats in the attic.
3. Their neighbors, Nate, Bryan, and Nikki, live in the gray house across the street.
4. They used to live in Michigan before they moved to Maryland.
5. Nate, Nikki, Sabrina, and Tasha take the bus to Bellevue Elementary School.
6. Mrs. Cullen took their litter of puppies to Miller Vet Hospital for shots.

Circle each pronoun or reflexive pronoun in the sentences below.

1. Nate reminded himself to call Sabrina on Monday.
2. He needed to tell her about a club meeting.
3. It started at 4:00.
4. We can walk there ourselves, he thought.
5. "I am glad that she and I are neighbors!"

Spectrum Language Arts
Grade 2

Review Chapter 1 Lessons 1–4
Grammar: Parts of Speech
15

15

Lesson 1.5 | Adjectives

Adjectives are words that describe. They give more information about nouns. Adjectives often answer the question **What kind?**

Kyle has a shirt.   Kyle has a **striped** shirt.

The adjective **striped** tells **what kind** of shirt Kyle has.

The adjectives in the sentences below are in bold.

Linh put the **yellow** flowers on the **wooden** table.
Jess has **curly, red** hair.
The **bright** moon shone in the **dark** sky.

Match It

Choose the adjective from the second column that best describes each noun in the first column. Write the letter of the adjective on the line. Some answers can be used twice.

1. the ___d___ sunshine   a. green
2. the ___c___ bird   b. rough
3. the ___a___ grass   c. chirping
4. the ___f___ squirrel   d. warm
5. the ___b___ bark of the tree e. noisy
6. the ___e___ lawnmower   f. furry

Tip Adjectives do not always come before nouns: **The sky is blue.** The adjective **blue** describes the noun **sky,** but it does not come right before it in the sentence.

Spectrum Language Arts
Grade 2
16

Chapter 1 Lesson 5
Grammar: Parts of Speech

16

Lesson 1.5 | Adjectives

Identify It

Read the sentences below. Circle the adjectives. Then, underline the nouns the adjectives describe.

Example: Kirsten made some cold, sweet lemonade.

1. A large raccoon lives in the woods near my house.
2. Raccoons have four legs and bushy tails.
3. They have black patches on their faces.
4. It looks like they are wearing funny masks.
5. Raccoons also have dark rings on their tails.
6. They sleep in warm dens in the winter.
7. Raccoons eat fresh fruit, eggs, and insects.

Try It

1. Write a sentence that describes an animal you have seen in the wild. Use two adjectives.

   Answers will vary.

2. Where do you think this animal lives? Write a sentence that describes the animal's home. Use two adjectives.

   Answers will vary.

Spectrum Language Arts
Grade 2

Chapter 1 Lesson 5
Grammar: Parts of Speech
17

17

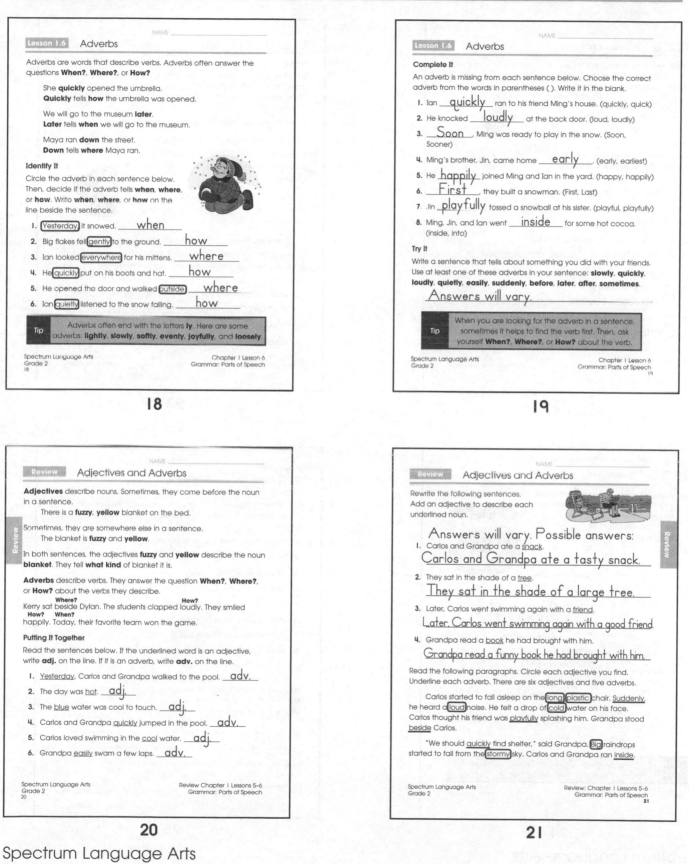

Page 18

Lesson 1.6 Adverbs

Adverbs are words that describe verbs. Adverbs often answer the questions **When?**, **Where?**, or **How?**

She **quickly** opened the umbrella.
Quickly tells **how** the umbrella was opened.

We will go to the museum **later**.
Later tells **when** we will go to the museum.

Maya ran **down** the street.
Down tells **where** Maya ran.

Identify It

Circle the adverb in each sentence below. Then, decide if the adverb tells **when**, **where**, or **how**. Write **when**, **where**, or **how** on the line beside the sentence.

1. Yesterday, it snowed. _____when_____
2. Big flakes fell gently to the ground. ___how___
3. Ian looked everywhere for his mittens. ___where___
4. He quickly put on his boots and hat. ___how___
5. He opened the door and walked outside. ___where___
6. Ian quietly listened to the snow falling. ___how___

Tip Adverbs often end with the letters **ly**. Here are some adverbs: **lightly**, **slowly**, **softly**, **evenly**, **joyfully**, and **loosely**.

Spectrum Language Arts
Grade 2
18

Chapter 1 Lesson 6
Grammar: Parts of Speech

18

Page 19

Lesson 1.6 Adverbs

Complete It

An adverb is missing from each sentence below. Choose the correct adverb from the words in parentheses ( ). Write it in the blank.

1. Ian ___quickly___ ran to his friend Ming's house. (quickly, quick)
2. He knocked ___loudly___ at the back door. (loud, loudly)
3. ___Soon___, Ming was ready to play in the snow. (Soon, Sooner)
4. Ming's brother, Jin, came home ___early___. (early, earliest)
5. He ___happily___ joined Ming and Ian in the yard. (happy, happily)
6. ___First___, they built a snowman. (First, Last)
7. Jin ___playfully___ tossed a snowball at his sister. (playful, playfully)
8. Ming, Jin, and Ian went ___inside___ for some hot cocoa. (inside, into)

Try It

Write a sentence that tells about something you did with your friends. Use at least one of these adverbs in your sentence: **slowly**, **quickly**, **loudly**, **quietly**, **easily**, **suddenly**, **before**, **later**, **after**, **sometimes**.

___Answers will vary.___

Tip When you are looking for the adverb in a sentence, sometimes it helps to find the verb first. Then, ask yourself **When?**, **Where?**, or **How?** about the verb.

Spectrum Language Arts
Grade 2

Chapter 1 Lesson 6
Grammar: Parts of Speech
19

19

Page 20

Review Adjectives and Adverbs

Adjectives describe nouns. Sometimes, they come before the noun in a sentence.
There is a **fuzzy**, **yellow** blanket on the bed.

Sometimes, they are somewhere else in a sentence.
The blanket is **fuzzy** and **yellow**.

In both sentences, the adjectives **fuzzy** and **yellow** describe the noun **blanket**. They tell **what kind** of blanket it is.

Adverbs describe verbs. They answer the question **When?**, **Where?**, or **How?** about the verbs they describe.

Where? How?
Kerry sat beside Dylan. The students clapped loudly. They smiled
How? When?
happily. Today, their favorite team won the game.

Putting It Together

Read the sentences below. If the underlined word is an adjective, write **adj.** on the line. If it is an adverb, write **adv.** on the line.

1. Yesterday, Carlos and Grandpa walked to the pool. ___adv.___
2. The day was hot. ___adj.___
3. The blue water was cool to touch. ___adj.___
4. Carlos and Grandpa quickly jumped in the pool. ___adv.___
5. Carlos loved swimming in the cool water. ___adj.___
6. Grandpa easily swam a few laps. ___adv.___

Spectrum Language Arts
Grade 2
20

Review Chapter 1 Lessons 5–6
Grammar: Parts of Speech

20

Page 21

Review Adjectives and Adverbs

Rewrite the following sentences. Add an adjective to describe each underlined noun.

___Answers will vary. Possible answers:___

1. Carlos and Grandpa ate a snack.
___Carlos and Grandpa ate a tasty snack.___

2. They sat in the shade of a tree.
___They sat in the shade of a large tree.___

3. Later, Carlos went swimming again with a friend.
___Later, Carlos went swimming again with a good friend.___

4. Grandpa read a book he had brought with him.
___Grandpa read a funny book he had brought with him.___

Read the following paragraphs. Circle each adjective you find. Underline each adverb. There are six adjectives and five adverbs.

Carlos started to fall asleep on the long, plastic chair. Suddenly, he heard a loud noise. He felt a drop of cold water on his face. Carlos thought his friend was playfully splashing him. Grandpa stood beside Carlos.

"We should quickly find shelter," said Grandpa. Big raindrops started to fall from the stormy sky. Carlos and Grandpa ran inside.

Spectrum Language Arts
Grade 2

Review: Chapter 1 Lessons 5–6
Grammar: Parts of Speech
21

21

Answer Key

Lesson 1.7 Statements

A **statement** is a sentence that begins with a capital letter and ends with a period. A statement tells the reader something. Each of the following sentences is a statement.

- My brother and I fly kites when we go to the beach.
- My kite is shaped like a diamond.
- It is purple, blue, and green.
- It has a long tail.

Rewrite It

Rewrite the following sentences. Each statement should begin with a capital letter and end with a period.

1. people have flown kites for thousands of years
   People have flown kites for thousands of years.

2. some kites are shaped like dragons or fish
   Some kites are shaped like dragons or fish.

3. others are shaped like birds
   Others are shaped like birds.

4. flying kites is a fun hobby
   Flying kites is a fun hobby.

Lesson 1.7 Statements

Proof It

Read the following paragraphs. Each statement should begin with a capital letter and end with a period. Use this proofreading mark (≡) under a letter to make it a capital. Use this proofreading mark (⊙) to add a period.

Example: nick and Matt made a kite shaped like a frog.

early kites were made in China. They were covered with silk. Other kites were covered with paper. the material covering the wooden sticks was sometimes painted by hand.

benjamin Franklin did experiments with kites. Alexander Graham Bell also used kites in his experiments.

today, kite festivals are held in many cities. people come from all around the world. They like to share their kites with other kite lovers. some kites are tiny. Others measure as much as one hundred feet.

Try It

1. What kind of kite would you make? Write a statement about it.
   Answers will vary.

2. Where would you fly the kite? Write a statement about it.
   Answers will vary.

Lesson 1.8 Questions

Questions are sentences that ask something. A question begins with a capital letter and ends with a question mark.

- Where are your shoes?
- Have you seen my hat?
- Did you put my mittens away?

Proof It

Read the letter below. Find the four periods that should be question marks. Write question marks in their place.

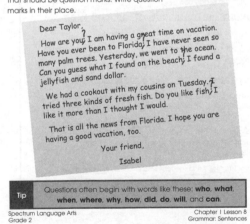

Dear Taylor,
How are you? I am having a great time on vacation. Have you ever been to Florida? I have never seen so many palm trees. Yesterday, we went to the ocean. Can you guess what I found on the beach? I found a jellyfish and sand dollar.

We had a cookout with my cousins on Tuesday. I tried three kinds of fresh fish. Do you like fish? I like it more than I thought I would.

That is all the news from Florida. I hope you are having a good vacation, too.

Your friend,

Isabel

Tip Questions often begin with words like these: **who**, **what**, **when**, **where**, **why**, **how**, **did**, **do**, **will**, and **can**.

Lesson 1.8 Questions

Complete It

Read the sentences that follow. If a sentence is a statement, add a period on the line. If a sentence is a question, add a question mark on the line.

1. Isabel and her family drove to Florida .
2. Do you know how long it took them to get there ?
3. They drove for three days .
4. Isabel has two sisters .
5. What did the girls do during the long drive ?
6. Did they play games in the car ?
7. Everyone in Isabel's family likes to sing .
8. Where will they go on vacation next year ?

Try It

On the lines below, write two questions you could ask Isabel about her vacation. Make sure each question begins with a capital letter and ends with a question mark.

Answers will vary.

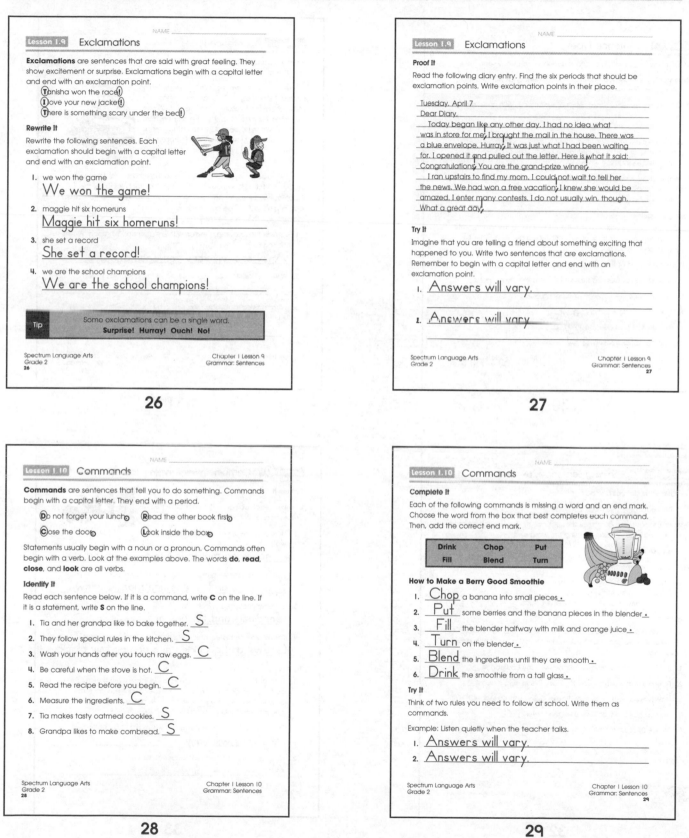

Lesson 1.9 Exclamations

Exclamations are sentences that are said with great feeling. They show excitement or surprise. Exclamations begin with a capital letter and end with an exclamation point.

(T)anisha won the race(!)

(I) love your new jacket(!)

(T)here is something scary under the bed(!)

Rewrite It

Rewrite the following sentences. Each exclamation should begin with a capital letter and end with an exclamation point.

1. we won the game

   We won the game!

2. maggie hit six homeruns

   Maggie hit six homeruns!

3. she set a record

   She set a record!

4. we are the school champions

   We are the school champions!

| Tip | Some exclamations can be a single word. **Surprise! Hurray! Ouch! No!** |

Spectrum Language Arts
Grade 2
26

Chapter 1 Lesson 9
Grammar: Sentences

26

Lesson 1.9 Exclamations

Proof It

Read the following diary entry. Find the six periods that should be exclamation points. Write exclamation points in their place.

Tuesday, April 7

Dear Diary,

Today began like any other day. I had no idea what was in store for me. I brought the mail in the house. There was a blue envelope. Hurray. It was just what I had been waiting for. I opened it and pulled out the letter. Here is what it said: Congratulations. You are the grand-prize winner. I ran upstairs to find my mom. I could not wait to tell her the news. We had won a free vacation. I knew she would be amazed. I enter many contests. I do not usually win, though. What a great day.

Try It

Imagine that you are telling a friend about something exciting that happened to you. Write two sentences that are exclamations. Remember to begin with a capital letter and end with an exclamation point.

1. Answers will vary.

2. Answers will vary.

Spectrum Language Arts
Grade 2

Chapter 1 Lesson 9
Grammar: Sentences
27

27

Lesson 1.10 Commands

Commands are sentences that tell you to do something. Commands begin with a capital letter. They end with a period.

(D)o not forget your lunch(.)   (R)ead the other book first(.)

(C)lose the door(.)   (L)ook inside the box(.)

Statements usually begin with a noun or a pronoun. Commands often begin with a verb. Look at the examples above. The words **do**, **read**, **close**, and **look** are all verbs.

Identify It

Read each sentence below. If it is a command, write **C** on the line. If it is a statement, write **S** on the line.

1. Tia and her grandpa like to bake together. S
2. They follow special rules in the kitchen. S
3. Wash your hands after you touch raw eggs. C
4. Be careful when the stove is hot. C
5. Read the recipe before you begin. C
6. Measure the ingredients. C
7. Tia makes tasty oatmeal cookies. S
8. Grandpa likes to make cornbread. S

Spectrum Language Arts
Grade 2
28

Chapter 1 Lesson 10
Grammar: Sentences

28

Lesson 1.10 Commands

Complete It

Each of the following commands is missing a word and an end mark. Choose the word from the box that best completes each command. Then, add the correct end mark.

Drink	Chop	Put
Fill	Blend	Turn

How to Make a Berry Good Smoothie

1. Chop a banana into small pieces .
2. Put some berries and the banana pieces in the blender .
3. Fill the blender halfway with milk and orange juice .
4. Turn on the blender .
5. Blend the ingredients until they are smooth .
6. Drink the smoothie from a tall glass .

Try It

Think of two rules you need to follow at school. Write them as commands.

Example: Listen quietly when the teacher talks.

1. Answers will vary.
2. Answers will vary.

Spectrum Language Arts
Grade 2

Chapter 1 Lesson 10
Grammar: Sentences
29

29

Spectrum Language Arts
Grade 2

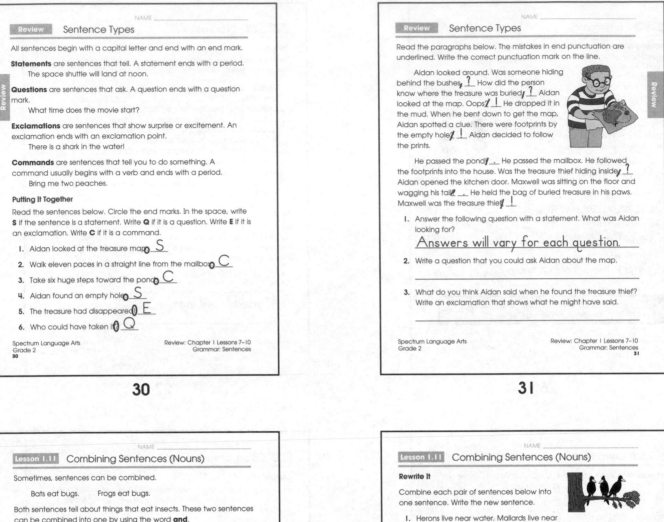

Page 30

Review | Sentence Types

All sentences begin with a capital letter and end with an end mark.

Statements are sentences that tell. A statement ends with a period.
   The space shuttle will land at noon.

Questions are sentences that ask. A question ends with a question mark.
   What time does the movie start?

Exclamations are sentences that show surprise or excitement. An exclamation ends with an exclamation point.
   There is a shark in the water!

Commands are sentences that tell you to do something. A command usually begins with a verb and ends with a period.
   Bring me two peaches.

Putting It Together

Read the sentences below. Circle the end marks. In the space, write **S** if the sentence is a statement. Write **Q** if it is a question. Write **E** if it is an exclamation. Write **C** if it is a command.

1. Aidan looked at the treasure map. **S**
2. Walk eleven paces in a straight line from the mailbox. **C**
3. Take six huge steps toward the pond. **C**
4. Aidan found an empty hole. **S**
5. The treasure had disappeared! **E**
6. Who could have taken it? **Q**

Spectrum Language Arts
Grade 2
30

Review: Chapter 1 Lessons 7–10
Grammar: Sentences

Page 31

Review | Sentence Types

Read the paragraphs below. The mistakes in end punctuation are underlined. Write the correct punctuation mark on the line.

Aidan looked around. Was someone hiding behind the bushes **?** How did the person know where the treasure was buried **?** Aidan looked at the map. Oops **!** He dropped it in the mud. When he bent down to get the map, Aidan spotted a clue. There were footprints by the empty hole **!** Aidan decided to follow the prints.

He passed the pond **.** He passed the mailbox. He followed the footprints into the house. Was the treasure thief hiding inside **?** Aidan opened the kitchen door. Maxwell was sitting on the floor and wagging his tail **.** He held the bag of buried treasure in his paws. Maxwell was the treasure thief **!**

1. Answer the following question with a statement. What was Aidan looking for?
   Answers will vary for each question.

2. Write a question that you could ask Aidan about the map.

3. What do you think Aidan said when he found the treasure thief? Write an exclamation that shows what he might have said.

Spectrum Language Arts
Grade 2

Review: Chapter 1 Lessons 7–10
Grammar: Sentences
31

Page 32

Lesson 1.11 | Combining Sentences (Nouns)

Sometimes, sentences can be combined.

   Bats eat bugs.   Frogs eat bugs.

Both sentences tell about things that eat insects. These two sentences can be combined into one by using the word **and**.

   Bats **and** frogs eat bugs.

Here is another example.

   Children like to go to the beach.
   Adults like to go to the beach.
   Children **and** adults like to go to the beach.

Identify It

Read each pair of sentences below. If the sentences can be joined with the word **and**, make a check mark (✓) on the line. If not, leave the line blank.

1. Blue jays visit my birdfeeder. Robins visit my birdfeeder. **✓**
2. Parrots live in warm places. Penguins live in cold places. ____
3. Hawks build nests on ledges. Eagles build nests on ledges. **✓**
4. Hummingbirds like flowers. Bees like flowers. **✓**
5. Geese fly south for the winter. Owls do not fly south in the winter. ____

Spectrum Language Arts
Grade 2
32

Chapter 1 Lesson 11
Grammar: Sentences

Page 33

Lesson 1.11 | Combining Sentences (Nouns)

Rewrite It

Combine each pair of sentences below into one sentence. Write the new sentence.

1. Herons live near water. Mallards live near water.
   Herons and mallards live near water.

2. Sparrows are mostly brown. Wrens are mostly brown.
   Sparrows and wrens are mostly brown.

3. Cardinals eat seeds. Finches eat seeds.
   Cardinals and finches eat seeds.

4. Crows are completely black. Grackles are completely black.
   Crows and grackles are completely black.

Try It

1. Think of two things that are the same in some way. They might be the same color or the same size. They might eat the same thing or like doing the same thing. Write a pair of sentences about the two things you chose.

   Example: Cats like to be petted.   Dogs like to be petted.
   Answers will vary.

2. Now, combine the two sentences you wrote into one.
   Answers will vary.

Spectrum Language Arts
Grade 2

Chapter 1 Lesson 11
Grammar: Sentences
33

Answer Key

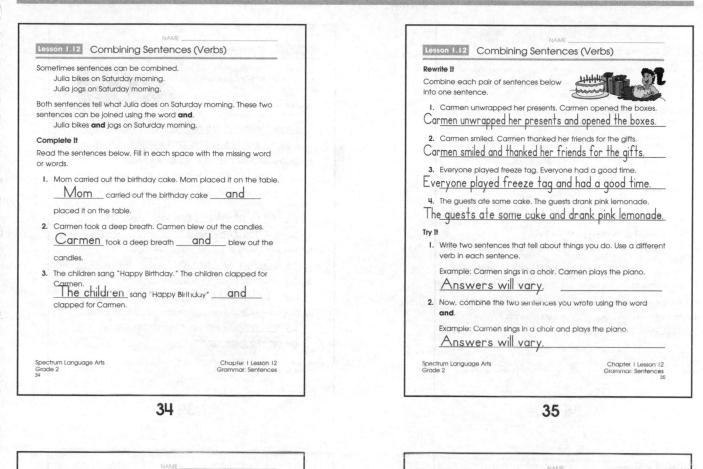

Lesson 1.12 Combining Sentences (Verbs)

Sometimes sentences can be combined.
    Julia bikes on Saturday morning.
    Julia jogs on Saturday morning.

Both sentences tell what Julia does on Saturday morning. These two sentences can be joined using the word **and**.
    Julia bikes **and** jogs on Saturday morning.

Complete It

Read the sentences below. Fill in each space with the missing word or words.

1. Mom carried out the birthday cake. Mom placed it on the table.
    <u>Mom</u> carried out the birthday cake <u>and</u>
    placed it on the table.

2. Carmen took a deep breath. Carmen blew out the candles.
    <u>Carmen</u> took a deep breath <u>and</u> blew out the
    candles.

3. The children sang "Happy Birthday." The children clapped for Carmen.
    <u>The children</u> sang "Happy Birthday" <u>and</u>
    clapped for Carmen.

Spectrum Language Arts
Grade 2
34

Chapter 1 Lesson 12
Grammar: Sentences

34

Lesson 1.12 Combining Sentences (Verbs)

Rewrite It

Combine each pair of sentences below into one sentence.

1. Carmen unwrapped her presents. Carmen opened the boxes.
    Carmen unwrapped her presents and opened the boxes.

2. Carmen smiled. Carmen thanked her friends for the gifts.
    Carmen smiled and thanked her friends for the gifts.

3. Everyone played freeze tag. Everyone had a good time.
    Everyone played freeze tag and had a good time.

4. The guests ate some cake. The guests drank pink lemonade.
    The guests ate some cake and drank pink lemonade.

Try It

1. Write two sentences that tell about things you do. Use a different verb in each sentence.

    Example: Carmen sings in a choir. Carmen plays the piano.
    <u>Answers will vary.</u>

2. Now, combine the two sentences you wrote using the word **and**.

    Example: Carmen sings in a choir and plays the piano.
    <u>Answers will vary.</u>

Spectrum Language Arts
Grade 2

Chapter 1 Lesson 12
Grammar: Sentences
35

35

Lesson 1.12 Combining Sentences (Adjectives)

Sometimes sentences can be combined.
    The wagon was red.   The wagon was shiny.

The adjectives **red** and **shiny** both describe **wagon**. These two sentences can be combined into one by using the word **and**.
    The wagon was red **and** shiny.

Here is another example.
    Danny has a new scooter.   The scooter is blue.

The adjectives **new** and **blue** describe Danny's scooter. The two sentences can be combined.
    Danny has a **new, blue** scooter.

Identify It

Read each pair of sentences below. If the adjectives in both sentences describe the same person or thing, the sentences can be combined. Make a check mark (✓) on the line if the two sentences can be combined.

1. Oliver's painting is bright. Oliver's painting is cheerful. <u>✓</u>

2. Oliver painted the flower garden. The garden was colorful. <u>✓</u>

3. Oliver's paintbrush is soft. Oliver's paints are new. <u>___</u>

4. The wall is large. The wall is white. <u>✓</u>

5. The tulips are red. The rosebushes are big. <u>___</u>

Spectrum Language Arts
Grade 2
36

Chapter 1 Lesson 13
Grammar: Sentences

36

Lesson 1.13 Combining Sentences (Adjectives)

Rewrite It

Combine each pair of sentences below into one sentence.

1. The paints are shiny. The paints are wet.
    The paints are shiny and wet.

2. The afternoon is warm. The afternoon is sunny.
    The afternoon is warm and sunny.

3. Oliver's paintings are beautiful. Oliver's paintings are popular.
    Oliver's paintings are beautiful and popular.

4. The red tulips are Oliver's favorite. The tulips are pretty.
    The pretty, red tulips are Oliver's favorite.

Try It

1. Write two sentences that describe your hair. Use a different adjective in each sentence.

    Example: My hair is red.   My hair is curly.
    <u>Answers will vary.</u>

2. Now write a sentence that combines the two sentences you wrote.

    Example: My hair is red and curly.
    <u>Answers will vary.</u>

Spectrum Language Arts
Grade 2

Chapter 1 Lesson 13
Grammar: Sentences
37

37

Spectrum Language Arts
Grade 2

Answer Key

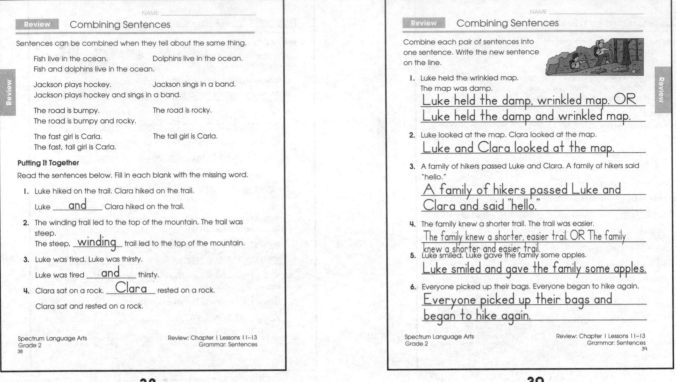

Page 38

Review Combining Sentences

Sentences can be combined when they tell about the same thing.

Fish live in the ocean.   Dolphins live in the ocean.
Fish and dolphins live in the ocean.

Jackson plays hockey.   Jackson sings in a band.
Jackson plays hockey and sings in a band.

The road is bumpy.   The road is rocky.
The road is bumpy and rocky.

The fast girl is Carla.   The tall girl is Carla.
The fast, tall girl is Carla.

Putting It Together

Read the sentences below. Fill in each blank with the missing word.

1. Luke hiked on the trail. Clara hiked on the trail.

    Luke ___and___ Clara hiked on the trail.

2. The winding trail led to the top of the mountain. The trail was steep.

    The steep, __winding__ trail led to the top of the mountain.

3. Luke was tired. Luke was thirsty.

    Luke was tired ___and___ thirsty.

4. Clara sat on a rock. __Clara__ rested on a rock.

    Clara sat and rested on a rock.

Spectrum Language Arts
Grade 2
38

Review: Chapter 1 Lessons 11–13
Grammar: Sentences

Page 39

Review Combining Sentences

Combine each pair of sentences into one sentence. Write the new sentence on the line.

1. Luke held the wrinkled map.
   The map was damp.

   Luke held the damp, wrinkled map. OR Luke held the damp and wrinkled map.

2. Luke looked at the map. Clara looked at the map.

   Luke and Clara looked at the map.

3. A family of hikers passed Luke and Clara. A family of hikers said "hello."

   A family of hikers passed Luke and Clara and said "hello."

4. The family knew a shorter trail. The trail was easier.

   The family knew a shorter, easier trail. OR The family knew a shorter and easier trail.

5. Luke smiled. Luke gave the family some apples.

   Luke smiled and gave the family some apples.

6. Everyone picked up their bags. Everyone began to hike again.

   Everyone picked up their bags and began to hike again.

Spectrum Language Arts
Grade 2

Review: Chapter 1 Lessons 11–13
Grammar: Sentences
39

Page 40

Chapter 2 Mechanics
Lesson 2.1 Capitalizing the First Word in a Sentence

All sentences begin with a capital letter. A capital letter is a sign to the reader that a new sentence is starting.

Marisol colored the leaves with a green crayon.
Alexander loves to dance.

The bus will arrive at three o'clock.
Is the book on the coffee table?

I love your backpack!
Raise your left hand.

Proof It

Read the paragraphs below. The first word of every sentence should begin with a capital letter. To show that a letter should be a capital, underline it three times (≡). Then, write the capital letter above it.

Example: <u>y</u>our socks don't match.

<u>T</u>ree trunks can tell the story of a tree's life. <u>a</u> slice of a tree trunk shows many rings. <u>a</u> tree adds a new ring every year. <u>e</u>ach ring has a light part and a dark part. <u>w</u>hen scientists look at the rings, they learn about the tree.

<u>t</u>he rings can tell how old a tree is. <u>t</u>hey can tell what the weather was like. <u>i</u>f there was a fire or a flood, the rings will show it. <u>t</u>rees cannot talk, but they do tell stories.

Spectrum Language Arts
Grade 2
40

Chapter 2 Lesson 1
Mechanics: Capitalization

Page 41

Lesson 2.1 Capitalizing the First Word in a Sentence

Rewrite It

Rewrite each sentence below. Make sure your sentences begin with a capital letter.

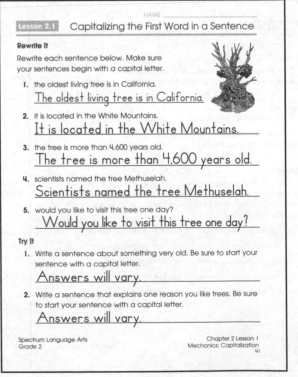

1. the oldest living tree is in California.

   The oldest living tree is in California.

2. it is located in the White Mountains.

   It is located in the White Mountains.

3. the tree is more than 4,600 years old.

   The tree is more than 4,600 years old.

4. scientists named the tree Methuselah.

   Scientists named the tree Methuselah.

5. would you like to visit this tree one day?

   Would you like to visit this tree one day?

Try It

1. Write a sentence about something very old. Be sure to start your sentence with a capital letter.

   Answers will vary.

2. Write a sentence that explains one reason you like trees. Be sure to start your sentence with a capital letter.

   Answers will vary.

Spectrum Language Arts
Grade 2

Chapter 2 Lesson 1
Mechanics: Capitalization
41

Answer Key

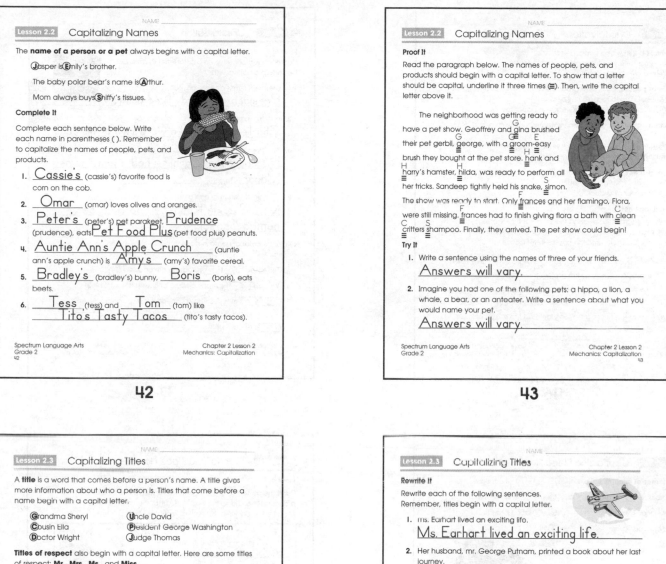

Lesson 2.2 Capitalizing Names

The **name of a person or a pet** always begins with a capital letter.

(J)asper is (E)mily's brother.

The baby polar bear's name is (A)rthur.

Mom always buys (S)hiffy's tissues.

Complete It

Complete each sentence below. Write each name in parentheses ( ). Remember to capitalize the names of people, pets, and products.

1. **Cassie's** (cassie's) favorite food is corn on the cob.

2. **Omar** (omar) loves olives and oranges.

3. **Peter's** (peter's) pet parakeet, **Prudence** (prudence), eats **Pet Food Plus** (pet food plus) peanuts.

4. **Auntie Ann's Apple Crunch** (auntie ann's apple crunch) is **Amy's** (amy's) favorite cereal.

5. **Bradley's** (bradley's) bunny, **Boris** (boris), eats beets.

6. **Tess** (tess) and **Tom** (tom) like **Tito's Tasty Tacos** (tito's tasty tacos).

Spectrum Language Arts
Grade 2
42

Chapter 2 Lesson 2
Mechanics: Capitalization

42

Lesson 2.2 Capitalizing Names

Proof It

Read the paragraph below. The names of people, pets, and products should begin with a capital letter. To show that a letter should be capital, underline it three times (≡). Then, write the capital letter above it.

The neighborhood was getting ready to have a pet show. Geoffrey and gina (G) brushed their pet gerbil, george (G), with a groom-easy (E) brush they bought at the pet store. hank (H) and harry's (H) hamster, hilda (H), was ready to perform all her tricks. Sandeep tightly held his snake, simon (S). The show was ready to start. Only frances (F) and her flamingo, Flora, were still missing. frances (F) had to finish giving flora (F) a bath with clean (C) critters shampoo (C S). Finally, they arrived. The pet show could begin!

Try It

1. Write a sentence using the names of three of your friends.

   Answers will vary.

2. Imagine you had one of the following pets: a hippo, a lion, a whale, a bear, or an anteater. Write a sentence about what you would name your pet.

   Answers will vary.

Spectrum Language Arts
Grade 2

Chapter 2 Lesson 2
Mechanics: Capitalization
43

43

Lesson 2.3 Capitalizing Titles

A **title** is a word that comes before a person's name. A title gives more information about who a person is. Titles that come before a name begin with a capital letter.

(G)randma Sheryl   (U)ncle David
(C)ousin Ella   (P)resident George Washington
(D)octor Wright   (J)udge Thomas

Titles of respect also begin with a capital letter. Here are some titles of respect: **Mr.**, **Mrs.**, **Ms.**, and **Miss.**

(M)r. Garza   (M)iss Sullivan   (M)s. Romano   (M)rs. Chun

Proof It

Read the diary entry below. All titles should begin with a capital letter. To show that a letter should be a capital, underline it three times (≡). Then, write the capital letter above it.

Dear Diary,

Last night, I went to a play with aunt (A) Sonia and uncle (U) Pat. I sat next to cousin (C) Fiona and cousin (C) Nora. The play was about ms. (M) Amelia Earhart, the first woman to fly across the Atlantic Ocean alone. ms. (M) Earhart led an exciting life. She even met president (P) Roosevelt.

After the play, I met Aunt Sonia's friend, mrs. (M) Angley. She played the role of ms. (M) Earhart. I also met mr. (M) Roche. He played the role of president (P) Roosevelt. He was very kind and funny.

Spectrum Language Arts
Grade 2
44

Chapter 2 Lesson 3
Mechanics: Capitalization

44

Lesson 2.3 Capitalizing Titles

Rewrite It

Rewrite each of the following sentences. Remember, titles begin with a capital letter.

1. ms. Earhart lived an exciting life.

   Ms. Earhart lived an exciting life.

2. Her husband, mr. George Putnam, printed a book about her last journey.

   Her husband, Mr. George Putnam, printed a book about her last journey.

3. grandpa Leo gave aunt Sonia the book.

   Grandpa Leo gave Aunt Sonia the book.

4. grandma Lucy read it last year.

   Grandma Lucy read it last year.

5. She also read a book about mrs. Roosevelt.

   She also read a book about Mrs. Roosevelt.

Try It

What person from history would you like to meet? Use the person's title in your answer.

Answers will vary.

Spectrum Language Arts
Grade 2

Chapter 2 Lesson 3
Mechanics: Capitalization
45

45

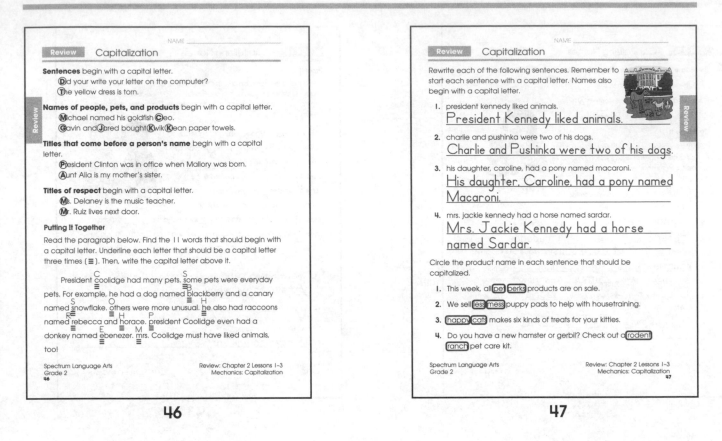

Page 46

Review — Capitalization

NAME _____

Sentences begin with a capital letter.
(D)id your write your letter on the computer?
(T)he yellow dress is torn.

Names of people, pets, and products begin with a capital letter.
(M)ichael named his goldfish (C)leo.
(G)avin and (J)ared bought (K)wik (K)lean paper towels.

Titles that come before a person's name begin with a capital letter.
(P)resident Clinton was in office when Mallory was born.
(A)unt Alia is my mother's sister.

Titles of respect begin with a capital letter.
(M)s. Delaney is the music teacher.
(M)r. Ruiz lives next door.

Putting It Together

Read the paragraph below. Find the 11 words that should begin with a capital letter. Underline each letter that should be a capital letter three times (≡). Then, write the capital letter above it.

President coolidge had many pets. some pets were everyday
pets. For example, he had a dog named blackberry and a canary
named snowflake. others were more unusual. he also had raccoons
named rebecca and horace. president Coolidge even had a
donkey named ebenezer. mrs. Coolidge must have liked animals,
too!

Spectrum Language Arts
Grade 2
46
Review: Chapter 2 Lessons 1–3
Mechanics: Capitalization

Page 47

Review — Capitalization

NAME _____

Rewrite each of the following sentences. Remember to start each sentence with a capital letter. Names also begin with a capital letter.

1. president kennedy liked animals.
President Kennedy liked animals.

2. charlie and pushinka were two of his dogs.
Charlie and Pushinka were two of his dogs.

3. his daughter, caroline, had a pony named macaroni.
His daughter, Caroline, had a pony named Macaroni.

4. mrs. jackie kennedy had a horse named sardar.
Mrs. Jackie Kennedy had a horse named Sardar.

Circle the product name in each sentence that should be capitalized.

1. This week, all (pet berks) products are on sale.

2. We sell (less mess) puppy pads to help with housetraining.

3. (happy cats) makes six kinds of treats for your kitties.

4. Do you have a new hamster or gerbil? Check out a (rodent ranch) pet care kit.

Spectrum Language Arts
Grade 2
Review: Chapter 2 Lessons 1–3
Mechanics: Capitalization
47

Page 48

Lesson 2.4 — Capitalizing Place Names

NAME _____

The **names of special places** always begin with a capital letter.

(R)ockwell (E)lementary (S)chool   (G)arner (S)cience (M)useum
(O)rlando, (F)lorida   (B)ay (V)illage (L)ibrary
(M)ississippi (R)iver   (M)ars
(D)onovan (S)treet   (F)rance

Complete It

Complete each sentence below with the word in parentheses ( ). Remember, special places begin with a capital letter.

1. My family left Charlotte,
North Carolina (north carolina), yesterday morning.

2. We waved good-bye to our house on
Clancy Avenue (clancy avenue).

3. We passed Washington Elementary School (washington elementary school).

4. Then, we crossed Hilliard Bridge (hilliard bridge).

5. We were on our way across the United States (united states)!

Spectrum Language Arts
Grade 2
48
Chapter 2 Lesson 4
Mechanics: Capitalization

Page 49

Lesson 2.4 — Capitalizing Place Names

NAME _____

Proof It

Read the postcard below. Find the 15 words that should begin with a capital letter. Underline each letter that should be a capital three times (≡). Then, write the capital letter above it.

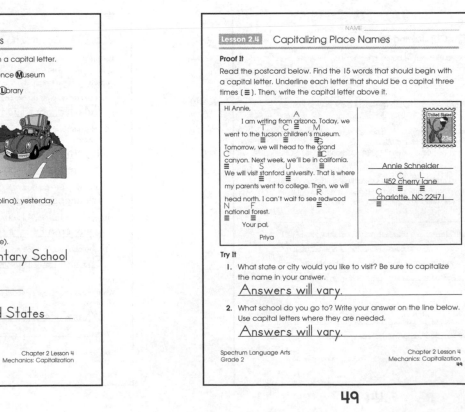

Hi Annie,
I am writing from arizona. Today, we went to the tucson children's museum. Tomorrow, we will head to the grand canyon. Next week, we'll be in california. We will visit stanford university. That is where my parents went to college. Then, we will head north. I can't wait to see redwood national forest.
Your pal,
Priya

Annie Schneider
452 cherry lane
Charlotte, NC 22471

Try It

1. What state or city would you like to visit? Be sure to capitalize the name in your answer.
Answers will vary.

2. What school do you go to? Write your answer on the line below. Use capital letters where they are needed.
Answers will vary.

Spectrum Language Arts
Grade 2
49
Chapter 2 Lesson 4
Mechanics: Capitalization

Page 50

Lesson 2.5 Capitalizing Days, Months, and Holidays

The **days of the week** each begin with a capital letter.
(M)onday, (T)uesday, (W)ednesday, (T)hursday, (F)riday, (S)aturday, (S)unday

The **months of the year** are also capitalized.
(J)anuary, (M)ay, (J)une, (O)ctober,

The **names of holidays** begin with a capital letter.
(C)hristmas, (T)hanksgiving, (V)alentine's (D)ay, (K)wanzaa

Proof It

Read the sentences below. Underline each letter that should be capital three times (≡). Then, write the capital letter above it.

1. I have to go to the doctor on <u>M</u>onday.
2. Softball practice starts on <u>T</u>uesday afternoon.
3. <u>W</u>ednesday is Miguel's birthday.
4. There is no school on <u>P</u>residents' <u>D</u>ay.
5. I will go to my piano lesson on <u>F</u>riday.
6. We will go to the grocery store on <u>S</u>aturday morning.
7. Grandma will visit during <u>H</u>anukkah.

Mon.	Tues.	Wed.	Thurs.	Fri.	Sat.	Sun.
1 doctor appointment	2 softball practice	3 Miguel's birthday	4 presidents' day	5 piano practice	6 grocery shopping	7 hanukkah

50

Page 51

Lesson 2.5 Capitalizing Days, Months, and Holidays

Rewrite It

The Brandon family keeps a list of important holidays and dates. Read the list. If the date or holiday is written correctly, make a check mark (✓) on the line. If it is not written correctly, rewrite it.

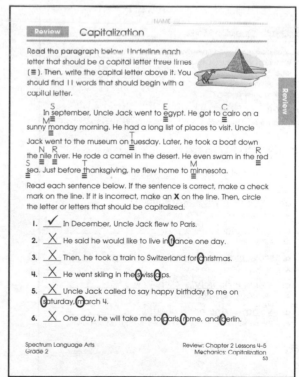

Ella's birthday	january 20	January 20
valentine's Day	February 14	Valentine's Day
Shane's party	May 11	✓
Kahlil's first birthday	june 22	June 22
the Cheswicks' trip	july 18	July 18
thanksgiving	November 23	Thanksgiving
Tyson's birthday	december 29	December 29

Try It

1. Write a sentence about something that happened this week. Tell what day of the week it happened.

   <u>Answers will vary.</u>

2. What is your favorite holiday? Why?

   <u>Answers will vary.</u>

51

Page 52

Review Capitalization

The **names of special places** always begin with a capital letter.
(W)estwood Hospital   (B)razil
(L)inden (S)treet   (P)ittsburgh, (P)ennsylvania
(L)ake (E)rie   (H)ampton (H)igh (S)chool

The **names of days, months, and holidays** always begin with a capital letter.
Summer vacation starts on (T)hursday, (J)une 9.
We first met in (O)ctober.
We always have a cookout on (L)abor (D)ay.

Putting It Together

Read the directions below. Complete each sentence with the word or words in parentheses ( ). Remember, special places begin with a capital letter.

- Take <u>Maple Street</u> (maple street) to <u>Oak Lane</u> (oak lane), and turn left.
- You will pass <u>Wintergreen School</u> (wintergreen school).
- Turn left on <u>Westbury Avenue</u> (westbury avenue).
- In about a mile, you will see <u>Lane Pool</u> (lane pool).
- Turn right on <u>Pine Hill Drive</u> (pine hill drive).
- Cross <u>Stony Creek</u> (stony creek), and continue for two miles.
- You will see a <u>Michigan</u> (michigan) flag by the front door of our house.

52

Page 53

Review Capitalization

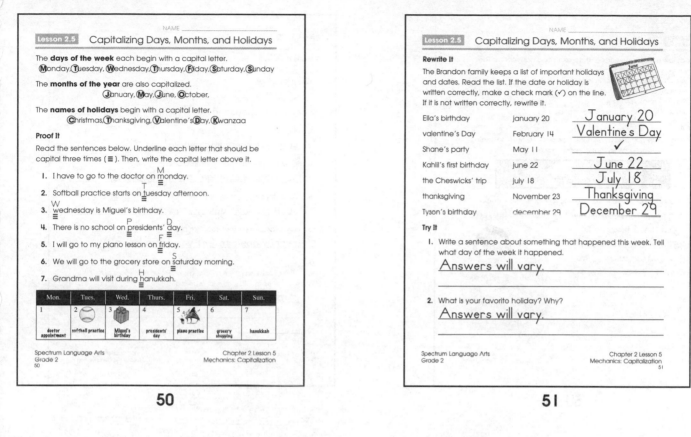

Read the paragraph below. Underline each letter that should be a capital letter three times (≡). Then, write the capital letter above it. You should find 11 words that should begin with a capital letter.

In <u>S</u>eptember, Uncle Jack went to <u>E</u>gypt. He got to <u>C</u>airo on a sunny <u>M</u>onday morning. He had a long list of places to visit. Uncle Jack went to the museum on <u>T</u>uesday. Later, he took a boat down the <u>N</u>ile <u>R</u>iver. He rode a camel in the desert. He even swam in the red <u>S</u>ea. Just before <u>T</u>hanksgiving, he flew home to <u>M</u>innesota.

Read each sentence below. If the sentence is correct, make a check mark on the line. If it is incorrect, make an **X** on the line. Then, circle the letter or letters that should be capitalized.

1. <u>✓</u> In December, Uncle Jack flew to Paris.
2. <u>X</u> He said he would like to live in (f)rance one day.
3. <u>X</u> Then, he took a train to Switzerland for (c)hristmas.
4. <u>X</u> He went skiing in the (s)wiss (a)lps.
5. <u>X</u> Uncle Jack called to say happy birthday to me on (s)aturday, (m)arch 4.
6. <u>X</u> One day, he will take me to (p)aris, (r)ome, and (b)erlin.

53

Answer Key

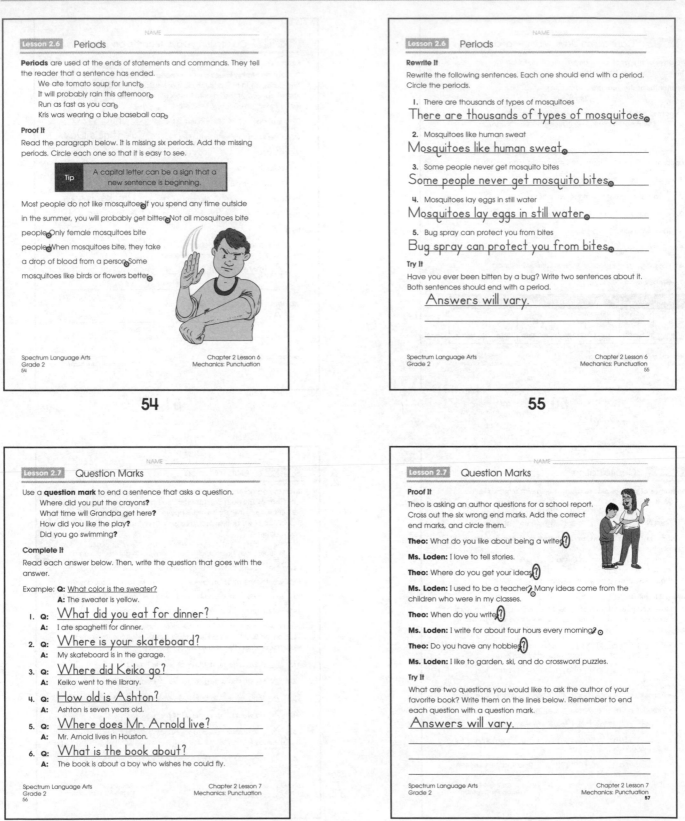

Lesson 2.6 Periods

Periods are used at the ends of statements and commands. They tell the reader that a sentence has ended.

We ate tomato soup for lunch.
It will probably rain this afternoon.
Run as fast as you can.
Kris was wearing a blue baseball cap.

Proof It

Read the paragraph below. It is missing six periods. Add the missing periods. Circle each one so that it is easy to see.

| Tip | A capital letter can be a sign that a new sentence is beginning. |

Most people do not like mosquitoes. If you spend any time outside in the summer, you will probably get bitten. Not all mosquitoes bite people. Only female mosquitoes bite people. When mosquitoes bite, they take a drop of blood from a person. Some mosquitoes like birds or flowers better.

Chapter 2 Lesson 6
Mechanics: Punctuation

54

Lesson 2.6 Periods

Rewrite It

Rewrite the following sentences. Each one should end with a period. Circle the periods.

1. There are thousands of types of mosquitoes

There are thousands of types of mosquitoes.

2. Mosquitoes like human sweat

Mosquitoes like human sweat.

3. Some people never get mosquito bites

Some people never get mosquito bites.

4. Mosquitoes lay eggs in still water

Mosquitoes lay eggs in still water.

5. Bug spray can protect you from bites

Bug spray can protect you from bites.

Try It

Have you ever been bitten by a bug? Write two sentences about it. Both sentences should end with a period.

Answers will vary.

Chapter 2 Lesson 6
Mechanics: Punctuation
55

55

Lesson 2.7 Question Marks

Use a **question mark** to end a sentence that asks a question.

Where did you put the crayons**?**
What time will Grandpa get here**?**
How did you like the play**?**
Did you go swimming**?**

Complete It

Read each answer below. Then, write the question that goes with the answer.

Example: **Q:** What color is the sweater?
A: The sweater is yellow.

1. **Q:** What did you eat for dinner?
   A: I ate spaghetti for dinner.

2. **Q:** Where is your skateboard?
   A: My skateboard is in the garage.

3. **Q:** Where did Keiko go?
   A: Keiko went to the library.

4. **Q:** How old is Ashton?
   A: Ashton is seven years old.

5. **Q:** Where does Mr. Arnold live?
   A: Mr. Arnold lives in Houston.

6. **Q:** What is the book about?
   A: The book is about a boy who wishes he could fly.

Chapter 2 Lesson 7
Mechanics: Punctuation

56

Lesson 2.7 Question Marks

Proof It

Theo is asking an author questions for a school report. Cross out the six wrong end marks. Add the correct end marks, and circle them.

Theo: What do you like about being a writer**?**

Ms. Loden: I love to tell stories.

Theo: Where do you get your ideas**?**

Ms. Loden: I used to be a teacher. Many ideas come from the children who were in my classes.

Theo: When do you write**?**

Ms. Loden: I write for about four hours every morning.

Theo: Do you have any hobbies**?**

Ms. Loden: I like to garden, ski, and do crossword puzzles.

Try It

What are two questions you would like to ask the author of your favorite book? Write them on the lines below. Remember to end each question with a question mark.

Answers will vary.

Chapter 2 Lesson 7
Mechanics: Punctuation
57

57

Answer Key

Answer Key

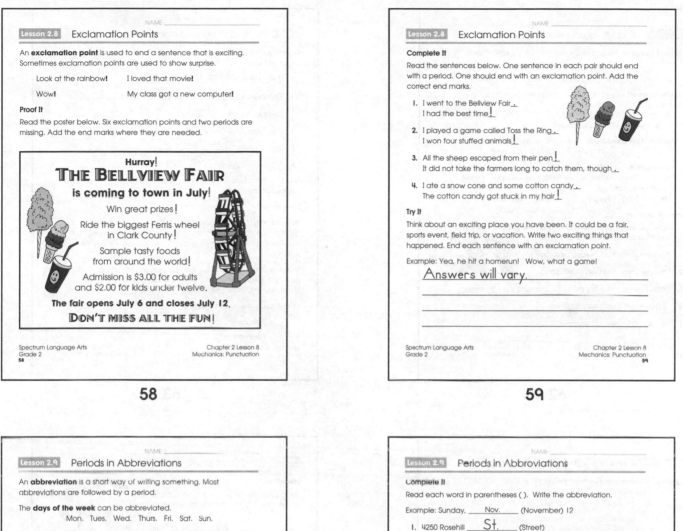

Lesson 2.8 Exclamation Points

An **exclamation point** is used to end a sentence that is exciting. Sometimes exclamation points are used to show surprise.

Look at the rainbow!   I loved that movie!

Wow!   My class got a new computer!

Proof It

Read the poster below. Six exclamation points and two periods are missing. Add the end marks where they are needed.

Hurray!
THE BELLVIEW FAIR
is coming to town in July!
Win great prizes!
Ride the biggest Ferris wheel in Clark County!
Sample tasty foods from around the world!
Admission is $3.00 for adults and $2.00 for kids under twelve.
The fair opens July 6 and closes July 12.
DON'T MISS ALL THE FUN!

Spectrum Language Arts
Grade 2
58

Chapter 2 Lesson 8
Mechanics: Punctuation

58

Lesson 2.8 Exclamation Points

Complete It

Read the sentences below. One sentence in each pair should end with a period. One should end with an exclamation point. Add the correct end marks.

1. I went to the Bellview Fair.
   I had the best time!

2. I played a game called Toss the Ring.
   I won four stuffed animals!

3. All the sheep escaped from their pen!
   It did not take the farmers long to catch them, though.

4. I ate a snow cone and some cotton candy.
   The cotton candy got stuck in my hair!

Try It

Think about an exciting place you have been. It could be a fair, sports event, field trip, or vacation. Write two exciting things that happened. End each sentence with an exclamation point.

Example: Yea, he hit a homerun! Wow, what a game!

Answers will vary.

Spectrum Language Arts
Grade 2

Chapter 2 Lesson 8
Mechanics: Punctuation
59

59

Lesson 2.9 Periods in Abbreviations

An **abbreviation** is a short way of writing something. Most abbreviations are followed by a period.

The **days of the week** can be abbreviated.
Mon. Tues. Wed. Thurs. Fri. Sat. Sun.

The **months of the year** also can be abbreviated. **May, June**, and **July** are not abbreviated because their names are so short.
Jan. Feb. Mar. Apr. Aug. Sept. Oct. Nov. Dec.

People's titles are almost always abbreviated when they come before a name.
Mrs. = missus Mr. = mister Dr. = doctor

Types of streets are abbreviated in addresses.
St. = street Ave. = avenue Dr. = drive Ln. = lane

Match It

Read each underlined word in the first column. Find the matching abbreviation in the second column. Write the letter of the abbreviation on the line.

1. _e_ 19052 Inglewood <u>Avenue</u>   a. Thurs.
2. _c_ <u>Doctor</u> Weinstein   b. Jan.
3. _a_ <u>Thursday</u> night   c. Dr.
4. _f_ <u>October</u> 15, 2006   d. Ln.
5. _d_ 18 Winding Creek <u>Lane</u>   e. Ave.
6. _b_ <u>January</u> 1, 2000   f. Oct.

Spectrum Language Arts
Grade 2
60

Chapter 2 Lesson 9
Mechanics: Punctuation

60

Lesson 2.9 Periods in Abbreviations

Complete It

Read each word in parentheses ( ). Write the abbreviation.

Example: Sunday, ___Nov.___ (November) 12

1. 4250 Rosehill ___St.___ (Street)
2. ___Mr.___ (Mister) Ortega
3. ___Apr.___ (April) 4, 2014
4. ___Feb.___ (February) 10, 1904
5. ___Wed.___ (Wednesday) morning
6. ___Mrs.___ (Missus) Antonivic
7. Beech ___Dr.___ (Drive)

Try It

1. Write your street address or school address using an abbreviation. Here are some other abbreviations you may need:

Rd. = road Blvd. = boulevard Ct. = court Cir. = circle

Answers will vary.

2. Write today's date using an abbreviation for the day of the week and month.

Answers will vary.

Spectrum Language Arts
Grade 2

Chapter 2 Lesson 9
Mechanics: Punctuation
61

61

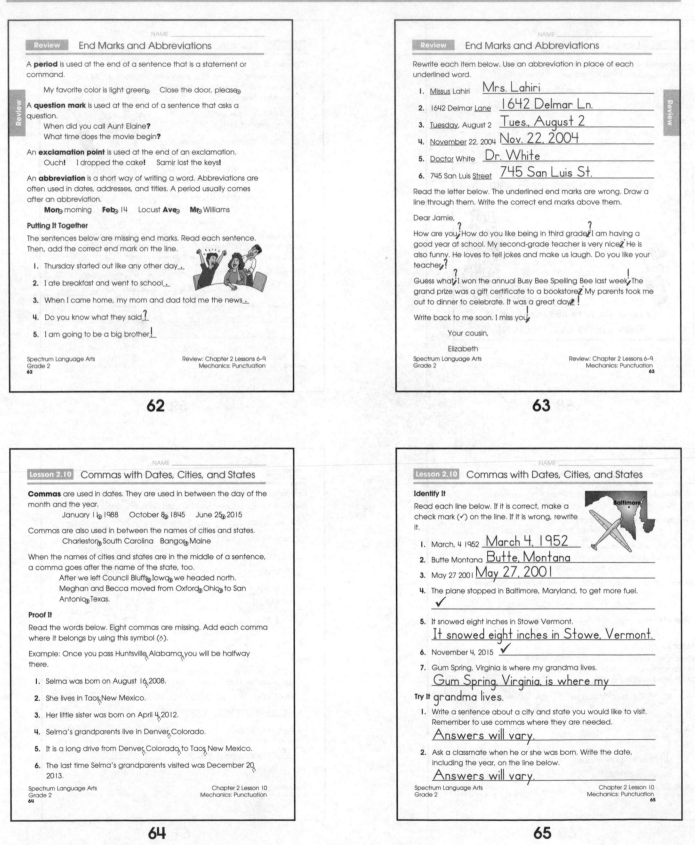

Review End Marks and Abbreviations

A **period** is used at the end of a sentence that is a statement or command.

My favorite color is light green.   Close the door, please.

A **question mark** is used at the end of a sentence that asks a question.

When did you call Aunt Elaine?
What time does the movie begin?

An **exclamation point** is used at the end of an exclamation.
Ouch!   I dropped the cake!   Samir lost the keys!

An **abbreviation** is a short way of writing a word. Abbreviations are often used in dates, addresses, and titles. A period usually comes after an abbreviation.

Mon. morning   Feb. 14   Locust Ave.   Mr. Williams

Putting It Together

The sentences below are missing end marks. Read each sentence. Then, add the correct end mark on the line.

1. Thursday started out like any other day.
2. I ate breakfast and went to school.
3. When I came home, my mom and dad told me the news.
4. Do you know what they said?
5. I am going to be a big brother!

Spectrum Language Arts
Grade 2
62

Review: Chapter 2 Lessons 6–9
Mechanics: Punctuation

62

Review End Marks and Abbreviations

Rewrite each item below. Use an abbreviation in place of each underlined word.

1. Missus Lahiri — Mrs. Lahiri
2. 1642 Delmar Lane — 1642 Delmar Ln.
3. Tuesday, August 2 — Tues., August 2
4. November 22, 2004 — Nov. 22, 2004
5. Doctor White — Dr. White
6. 745 San Luis Street — 745 San Luis St.

Read the letter below. The underlined end marks are wrong. Draw a line through them. Write the correct end marks above them.

Dear Jamie,

How are you? How do you like being in third grade? I am having a good year at school. My second-grade teacher is very nice. He is also funny. He loves to tell jokes and make us laugh. Do you like your teacher?

Guess what! I won the annual Busy Bee Spelling Bee last week. The grand prize was a gift certificate to a bookstore. My parents took me out to dinner to celebrate. It was a great day!

Write back to me soon. I miss you.

Your cousin,

Elizabeth

Spectrum Language Arts
Grade 2

Review: Chapter 2 Lessons 6–9
Mechanics: Punctuation
63

63

Lesson 2.10 Commas with Dates, Cities, and States

Commas are used in dates. They are used in between the day of the month and the year.

January 1, 1988   October 8, 1845   June 25, 2015

Commas are also used in between the names of cities and states.

Charleston, South Carolina   Bangor, Maine

When the names of cities and states are in the middle of a sentence, a comma goes after the name of the state, too.

After we left Council Bluffs, Iowa, we headed north.
Meghan and Becca moved from Oxford, Ohio, to San Antonio, Texas.

Proof It

Read the words below. Eight commas are missing. Add each comma where it belongs by using this symbol (∧).

Example: Once you pass Huntsville, Alabama, you will be halfway there.

1. Selma was born on August 16, 2008.
2. She lives in Taos, New Mexico.
3. Her little sister was born on April 4, 2012.
4. Selma's grandparents live in Denver, Colorado.
5. It is a long drive from Denver, Colorado, to Taos, New Mexico.
6. The last time Selma's grandparents visited was December 20, 2013.

Spectrum Language Arts
Grade 2
64

Chapter 2 Lesson 10
Mechanics: Punctuation

64

Lesson 2.10 Commas with Dates, Cities, and States

Identify It

Read each line below. If it is correct, make a check mark (✓) on the line. If it is wrong, rewrite it.

1. March, 4 1952 — March 4, 1952
2. Butte Montana — Butte, Montana
3. May 27 2001 — May 27, 2001
4. The plane stopped in Baltimore, Maryland, to get more fuel.
   ✓
5. It snowed eight inches in Stowe Vermont.
   It snowed eight inches in Stowe, Vermont.
6. November 4, 2015 ✓
7. Gum Spring, Virginia is where my grandma lives.
   Gum Spring, Virginia, is where my grandma lives.

Try It

1. Write a sentence about a city and state you would like to visit. Remember to use commas where they are needed.
   Answers will vary.
2. Ask a classmate when he or she was born. Write the date, including the year, on the line below.
   Answers will vary.

Spectrum Language Arts
Grade 2

Chapter 2 Lesson 10
Mechanics: Punctuation
65

65

Answer Key

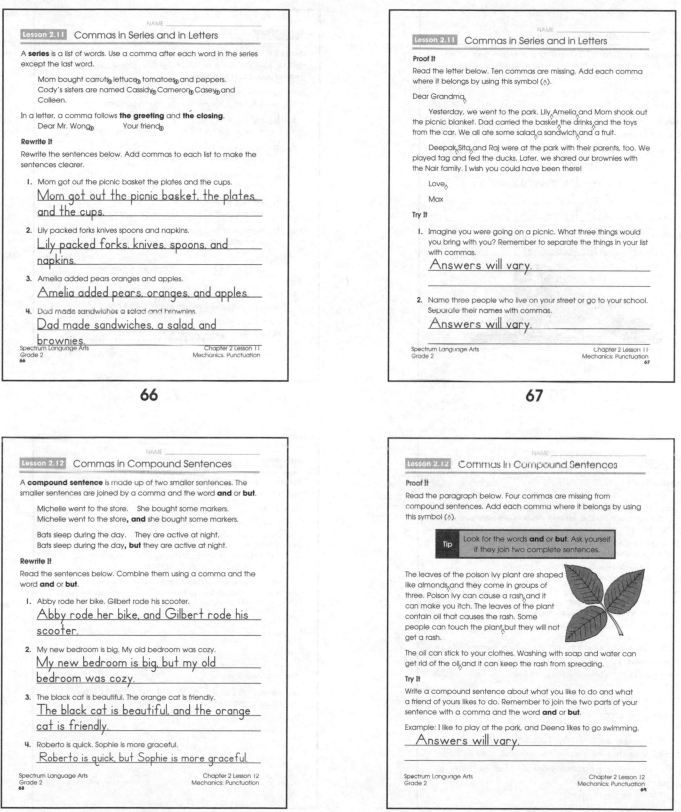

Lesson 2.11 Commas in Series and in Letters

NAME _____

A **series** is a list of words. Use a comma after each word in the series except the last word.

> Mom bought carrots, lettuce, tomatoes, and peppers.
> Cody's sisters are named Cassidy, Cameron, Casey, and Colleen.

In a letter, a comma follows **the greeting** and **the closing**.
> Dear Mr. Wong,   Your friend,

Rewrite It

Rewrite the sentences below. Add commas to each list to make the sentences clearer.

1. Mom got out the picnic basket the plates and the cups.

   Mom got out the picnic basket, the plates and the cups.

2. Lily packed forks knives spoons and napkins.

   Lily packed forks, knives, spoons, and napkins.

3. Amelia added pears oranges and apples.

   Amelia added pears, oranges, and apples.

4. Dad made sandwiches a salad and brownies.

   Dad made sandwiches, a salad, and brownies.

Spectrum Language Arts
Grade 2
66

Chapter 2 Lesson 11
Mechanics: Punctuation

Lesson 2.11 Commas in Series and in Letters

NAME _____

Proof It

Read the letter below. Ten commas are missing. Add each comma where it belongs by using this symbol (∧).

Dear Grandma,

Yesterday, we went to the park. Lily, Amelia, and Mom shook out the picnic blanket. Dad carried the basket, the drinks, and the toys from the car. We all ate some salad, a sandwich, and a fruit.

Deepak, Sita, and Raj were at the park with their parents, too. We played tag and fed the ducks. Later, we shared our brownies with the Nair family. I wish you could have been there!

Love,

Max

Try It

1. Imagine you were going on a picnic. What three things would you bring with you? Remember to separate the things in your list with commas.

   Answers will vary.

2. Name three people who live on your street or go to your school. Separate their names with commas.

   Answers will vary.

Spectrum Language Arts
Grade 2

Chapter 2 Lesson 11
Mechanics: Punctuation
67

Lesson 2.12 Commas in Compound Sentences

NAME _____

A **compound sentence** is made up of two smaller sentences. The smaller sentences are joined by a comma and the word **and** or **but**.

> Michelle went to the store.   She bought some markers.
> Michelle went to the store, **and** she bought some markers.

> Bats sleep during the day.   They are active at night.
> Bats sleep during the day, **but** they are active at night.

Rewrite It

Read the sentences below. Combine them using a comma and the word **and** or **but**.

1. Abby rode her bike. Gilbert rode his scooter.

   Abby rode her bike, and Gilbert rode his scooter.

2. My new bedroom is big. My old bedroom was cozy.

   My new bedroom is big, but my old bedroom was cozy.

3. The black cat is beautiful. The orange cat is friendly.

   The black cat is beautiful, and the orange cat is friendly.

4. Roberto is quick. Sophie is more graceful.

   Roberto is quick, but Sophie is more graceful.

Spectrum Language Arts
Grade 2
68

Chapter 2 Lesson 12
Mechanics: Punctuation

Lesson 2.12 Commas in Compound Sentences

NAME _____

Proof It

Read the paragraph below. Four commas are missing from compound sentences. Add each comma where it belongs by using this symbol (∧).

> **Tip** Look for the words **and** or **but**. Ask yourself if they join two complete sentences.

The leaves of the poison ivy plant are shaped like almonds, and they come in groups of three. Poison ivy can cause a rash, and it can make you itch. The leaves of the plant contain oil that causes the rash. Some people can touch the plant, but they will not get a rash.

The oil can stick to your clothes. Washing with soap and water can get rid of the oil, and it can keep the rash from spreading.

Try It

Write a compound sentence about what you like to do and what a friend of yours likes to do. Remember to join the two parts of your sentence with a comma and the word **and** or **but**.

Example: I like to play at the park, and Deena likes to go swimming.

Answers will vary.

Spectrum Language Arts
Grade 2

Chapter 2 Lesson 12
Mechanics: Punctuation
69

Answer Key

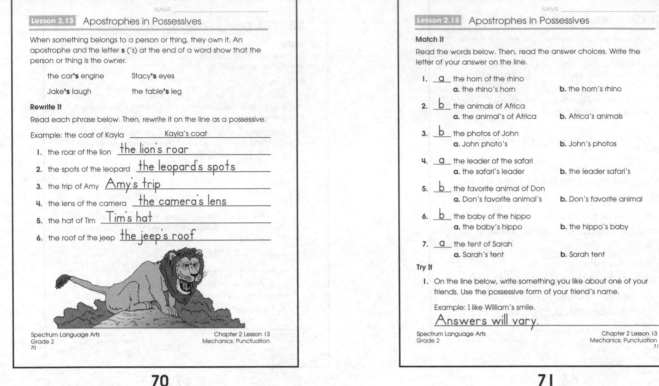

Page 70

Lesson 2.13 Apostrophes in Possessives

When something belongs to a person or thing, they own it. An apostrophe and the letter **s** ('s) at the end of a word show that the person or thing is the owner.

the car**'s** engine   Stacy**'s** eyes

Jake**'s** laugh   the table**'s** leg

Rewrite It

Read each phrase below. Then, rewrite it on the line as a possessive.

Example: the coat of Kayla _____ Kayla's coat _____

1. the roar of the lion   the lion's roar
2. the spots of the leopard   the leopard's spots
3. the trip of Amy   Amy's trip
4. the lens of the camera   the camera's lens
5. the hat of Tim   Tim's hat
6. the roof of the jeep   the jeep's roof

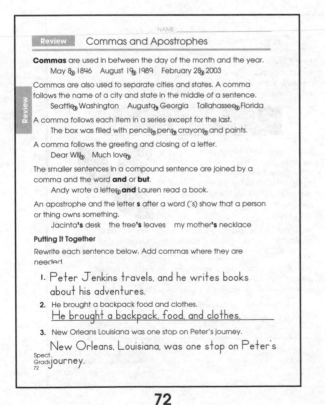

Spectrum Language Arts
Grade 2
70

Chapter 2 Lesson 13
Mechanics: Punctuation

70

Page 71

Lesson 2.13 Apostrophes in Possessives

Match It

Read the words below. Then, read the answer choices. Write the letter of your answer on the line.

1. _a_ the horn of the rhino
   a. the rhino's horn   b. the horn's rhino
2. _b_ the animals of Africa
   a. the animal's of Africa   b. Africa's animals
3. _b_ the photos of John
   a. John photo's   b. John's photos
4. _a_ the leader of the safari
   a. the safari's leader   b. the leader safari's
5. _b_ the favorite animal of Don
   a. Don's favorite animal's b. Don's favorite animal
6. _b_ the baby of the hippo
   a. the baby's hippo   b. the hippo's baby
7. _a_ the tent of Sarah
   a. Sarah's tent   b. Sarah tent

Try It

1. On the line below, write something you like about one of your friends. Use the possessive form of your friend's name.

   Example: I like William's smile.

   Answers will vary.

Spectrum Language Arts
Grade 2

Chapter 2 Lesson 13
Mechanics: Punctuation
71

71

Page 72

Review Commas and Apostrophes

Commas are used in between the day of the month and the year.
   May 8, 1846   August 19, 1989   February 28, 2003

Commas are also used to separate cities and states. A comma follows the name of a city and state in the middle of a sentence.
   Seattle, Washington   Augusta, Georgia   Tallahassee, Florida

A comma follows each item in a series except for the last.
   The box was filled with pencils, pens, crayons, and paints.

A comma follows the greeting and closing of a letter.
   Dear Will,   Much love,

The smaller sentences in a compound sentence are joined by a comma and the word **and** or **but**.
   Andy wrote a letter, **and** Lauren read a book.

An apostrophe and the letter **s** after a word ('s) show that a person or thing owns something.
   Jacinta**'s** desk   the tree**'s** leaves   my mother**'s** necklace

Putting It Together

Rewrite each sentence below. Add commas where they are needed.

1. Peter Jenkins travels, and he writes books about his adventures.
2. He brought a backpack food and clothes.
   He brought a backpack, food, and clothes.
3. New Orleans Louisiana was one stop on Peter's journey.
   New Orleans, Louisiana, was one stop on Peter's journey.

Spect.
Grade 2
72

72

Page 73

Review Commas and Apostrophes

Read the paragraphs below. There are 17 commas missing. Write each comma where it belongs.

Dear Quinn,

   I need to write a letter for school. I chose to write to you about Peter Jenkins. He was born on July 8, 1951 in Greenwich, Connecticut. Peter is best known for walking across America. He began his walk on October 15, 1973. He walked from Alfred, New York, to Florence, Oregon. His walk ended on January 18, 1979.

   Today, Peter lives on a farm in Spring Hill, Tennessee. His children are named Rebekah, Jedidiah, Luke, Aaron, Brooke, and Julianne. Peter likes to travel, write, and speak to people about his adventures.

   I hope you liked learning about Peter. I'll talk to you soon!

   Your friend,

   Eli

Read each sentence below. Rewrite the words in parentheses ( ) so they show ownership.

1. (The dog of Peter) Peter's dog , Cooper, walked across America with him.
2. (The people of America) America's people are very interesting to Peter Jenkins.
3. (The books of Peter) Peter's books are about the places he has traveled.

Spectrum Language Arts
Grade 2

Review: Chapter 2 Lessons 10–13
Mechanics: Punctuation
73

73

Spectrum Language Arts
Grade 2

Answer Key

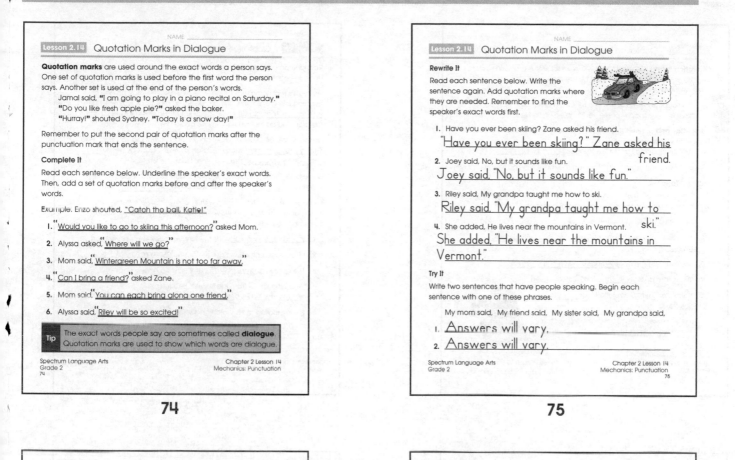

NAME _____

Lesson 2.14 Quotation Marks in Dialogue

Quotation marks are used around the exact words a person says. One set of quotation marks is used before the first word the person says. Another set is used at the end of the person's words.

Jamal said, **"I am going to play in a piano recital on Saturday."**

"Do you like fresh apple pie?" asked the baker.

"Hurray!" shouted Sydney. **"Today is a snow day!"**

Remember to put the second pair of quotation marks after the punctuation mark that ends the sentence.

Complete It

Read each sentence below. Underline the speaker's exact words. Then, add a set of quotation marks before and after the speaker's words.

Example: Enzo shouted, "Catch the ball, Katie!"

1. "Would you like to go to skiing this afternoon?" asked Mom.

2. Alyssa asked, "Where will we go?"

3. Mom said, "Wintergreen Mountain is not too far away."

4. "Can I bring a friend?" asked Zane.

5. Mom said, "You can each bring along one friend."

6. Alyssa said, "Riley will be so excited!"

> **Tip** The exact words people say are sometimes called **dialogue**. Quotation marks are used to show which words are dialogue.

Spectrum Language Arts
Grade 2
74

Chapter 2 Lesson 14
Mechanics: Punctuation

74

NAME _____

Lesson 2.14 Quotation Marks in Dialogue

Rewrite It

Read each sentence below. Write the sentence again. Add quotation marks where they are needed. Remember to find the speaker's exact words first.

1. Have you ever been skiing? Zane asked his friend.

"Have you ever been skiing?" Zane asked his friend.

2. Joey said, No, but it sounds like fun.

Joey said, "No, but it sounds like fun."

3. Riley said, My grandpa taught me how to ski.

Riley said, "My grandpa taught me how to ski."

4. She added, He lives near the mountains in Vermont.

She added, "He lives near the mountains in Vermont."

Try It

Write two sentences that have people speaking. Begin each sentence with one of these phrases.

My mom said, My friend said, My sister said, My grandpa said,

1. Answers will vary.

2. Answers will vary.

Spectrum Language Arts
Grade 2

Chapter 2 Lesson 14
Mechanics: Punctuation
75

75

NAME _____

Lesson 2.15 Titles of Books and Movies

The **titles of books and movies** are underlined in text. This lets the reader know that the underlined words are part of a title.

Cristina's favorite movie is Because of Winn-Dixie.

Harry wrote a book report on Nate the Great and the Musical Note.

Roald Dahl is the author of James and the Giant Peach.

I have seen the movie Aladdin four times.

Rewrite It

Read the sentences below. Rewrite each sentence and underline the title of each movie.

1. Tom Hanks was the voice of Woody in the movie Toy Story.

2. Mara Wilson played Matilda Wormwood in the movie Matilda.

3. In the movie Shrek, Cameron Diaz was the voice of Princess Fiona.

4. The movie Fly Away Home is based on a true story.

5. Harriet the Spy is the name of a book and a movie.

Spectrum Language Arts
Grade 2
76

Chapter 2 Lesson 15
Mechanics: Punctuation

76

NAME _____

Lesson 2.15 Titles of Books and Movies

Proof It

Read the paragraphs below. Find the five book titles, and underline them.

Jon Scieszka (say **shez ka**) is a popular author. He has written many books for children. He is best known for his book The Stinky Cheese Man and Other Fairly Stupid Tales. Jon has always loved books. Dr. Seuss's famous book Green Eggs and Ham made Jon feel like he could be a writer one day.

In 1989, Jon wrote The True Story of the Three Little Pigs. Many children think his books are very funny. They also like the pictures. Lane Smith draws the pictures for many of Jon's books. They worked together on the book Math Curse. Their book Science Verse is also popular.

Try It

1. Write the title of your favorite book on the line below. Remember to underline it.

Answers will vary.

2. What was the last movie you saw? Write the title on the line below. Remember to underline it.

Answers will vary.

Spectrum Language Arts
Grade 2

Chapter 2 Lesson 15
Mechanics: Punctuation
77

77

Answer Key

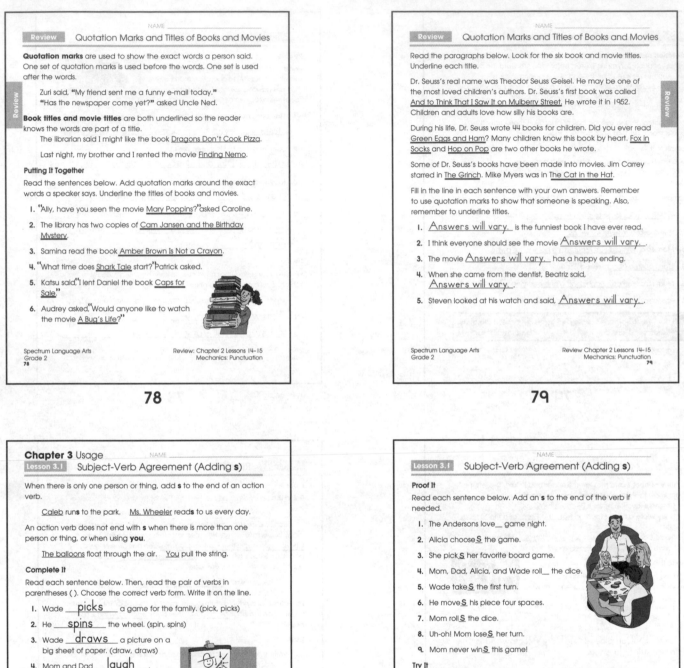

Page 78

Review Quotation Marks and Titles of Books and Movies

Quotation marks are used to show the exact words a person said. One set of quotation marks is used before the words. One set is used after the words.

Zuri said, "My friend sent me a funny e-mail today."

"Has the newspaper come yet?" asked Uncle Ned.

Book titles and movie titles are both underlined so the reader knows the words are part of a title.

The librarian said I might like the book Dragons Don't Cook Pizza.

Last night, my brother and I rented the movie Finding Nemo.

Putting It Together

Read the sentences below. Add quotation marks around the exact words a speaker says. Underline the titles of books and movies.

1. "Ally, have you seen the movie Mary Poppins?" asked Caroline.

2. The library has two copies of Cam Jansen and the Birthday Mystery.

3. Samina read the book Amber Brown Is Not a Crayon.

4. "What time does Shark Tale start?" Patrick asked.

5. Katsu said, "I lent Daniel the book Caps for Sale."

6. Audrey asked, "Would anyone like to watch the movie A Bug's Life?"

Spectrum Language Arts
Grade 2
78

Review: Chapter 2 Lessons 14–15
Mechanics: Punctuation

Page 79

Review Quotation Marks and Titles of Books and Movies

Read the paragraphs below. Look for the six book and movie titles. Underline each title.

Dr. Seuss's real name was Theodor Seuss Geisel. He may be one of the most loved children's authors. Dr. Seuss's first book was called And to Think That I Saw It on Mulberry Street. He wrote it in 1952. Children and adults love how silly his books are.

During his life, Dr. Seuss wrote 44 books for children. Did you ever read Green Eggs and Ham? Many children know this book by heart. Fox in Socks and Hop on Pop are two other books he wrote.

Some of Dr. Seuss's books have been made into movies. Jim Carrey starred in The Grinch. Mike Myers was in The Cat in the Hat.

Fill in the line in each sentence with your own answers. Remember to use quotation marks to show that someone is speaking. Also, remember to underline titles.

1. Answers will vary. is the funniest book I have ever read.

2. I think everyone should see the movie Answers will vary.

3. The movie Answers will vary. has a happy ending.

4. When she came from the dentist, Beatriz said, Answers will vary.

5. Steven looked at his watch and said, Answers will vary.

Spectrum Language Arts
Grade 2

Review Chapter 2 Lessons 14–15
Mechanics: Punctuation
79

Page 80

Chapter 3 Usage

Lesson 3.1 Subject-Verb Agreement (Adding **s**)

When there is only one person or thing, add **s** to the end of an action verb.

Caleb runs to the park. Ms. Wheeler reads to us every day.

An action verb does not end with **s** when there is more than one person or thing, or when using **you**.

The balloons float through the air. You pull the string.

Complete It

Read each sentence below. Then, read the pair of verbs in parentheses ( ). Choose the correct verb form. Write it on the line.

1. Wade _picks_ a game for the family. (pick, picks)

2. He _spins_ the wheel. (spin, spins)

3. Wade _draws_ a picture on a big sheet of paper. (draw, draws)

4. Mom and Dad _laugh_ (laugh, laughs)

5. Alicia _knows_ what the picture is. (know, knows)

6. She _rings_ the bell. (ring, rings)

7. Alicia and Wade _make_ a good team. (make, makes)

Spectrum Language Arts
Grade 2
80

Chapter 3 Lesson 1
Usage

Page 81

Lesson 3.1 Subject-Verb Agreement (Adding **s**)

Proof It

Read each sentence below. Add an **s** to the end of the verb if needed.

1. The Andersons love__ game night.

2. Alicia choose_S_ the game.

3. She pick_S_ her favorite board game.

4. Mom, Dad, Alicia, and Wade roll__ the dice.

5. Wade take_S_ the first turn.

6. He move_S_ his piece four spaces.

7. Mom roll_S_ the dice.

8. Uh-oh! Mom lose_S_ her turn.

9. Mom never win_S_ this game!

Try It

Use a pair of verbs from the box to write two sentences. One sentence should have only one person or thing. The other sentence should have more than one person or thing.

run, runs	play, plays
smile, smiles	throw, throws

1. Answers will vary.

2. Answers will vary.

Spectrum Language Arts
Grade 2
81

Chapter 3 Lesson 1
Usage

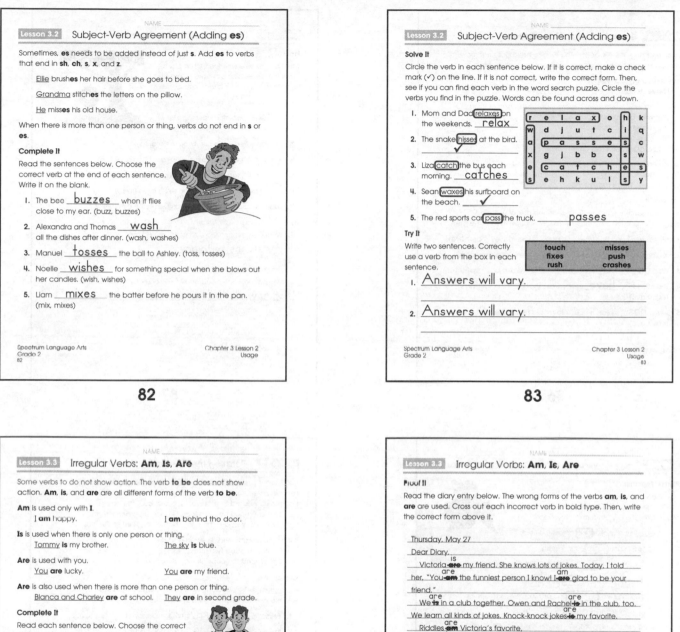

Answer Key

Lesson 3.2 Subject-Verb Agreement (Adding **es**)

Sometimes, **es** needs to be added instead of just **s**. Add **es** to verbs that end in **sh, ch, s, x,** and **z**.

Ellie brush**es** her hair before she goes to bed.

Grandma stitch**es** the letters on the pillow.

He miss**es** his old house.

When there is more than one person or thing, verbs do not end in **s** or **es**.

Complete It

Read the sentences below. Choose the correct verb at the end of each sentence. Write it on the blank.

1. The bee ___buzzes___ when it flies close to my ear. (buzz, buzzes)

2. Alexandra and Thomas ___wash___ all the dishes after dinner. (wash, washes)

3. Manuel ___tosses___ the ball to Ashley. (toss, tosses)

4. Noelle ___wishes___ for something special when she blows out her candles. (wish, wishes)

5. Liam ___mixes___ the batter before he pours it in the pan. (mix, mixes)

82

Lesson 3.2 Subject-Verb Agreement (Adding **es**)

Solve It

Circle the verb in each sentence below. If it is correct, make a check mark (✓) on the line. If it is not correct, write the correct form. Then, see if you can find each verb in the word search puzzle. Circle the verbs you find in the puzzle. Words can be found across and down.

1. Mom and Dad (relaxes) on the weekends. ___relax___

2. The snake (hisses) at the bird. ✓ _____

3. Liza (catch) the bus each morning. ___catches___

4. Sean (waxes) his surfboard on the beach. ✓

5. The red sports car (pass) the truck. ___passes___

r	e	l	a	x	o	h	k
w	d	j	u	t	c	i	q
a	(p	a	s	s	e	s)	c
x	g	j	b	b	o	s	w
e	(c	a	t	c	h	e	s)
	e	h	k	u	l	s	y

Try It

Write two sentences. Correctly use a verb from the box in each sentence.

touch	misses
fixes	push
rush	crashes

1. ___Answers will vary.___

2. ___Answers will vary.___

83

Lesson 3.3 Irregular Verbs: **Am, Is, Are**

Some verbs to do not show action. The verb **to be** does not show action. **Am, is,** and **are** are all different forms of the verb **to be**.

Am is used only with **I**.
I **am** happy.   I **am** behind the door.

Is is used when there is only one person or thing.
Tommy **is** my brother.   The sky **is** blue.

Are is used with you.
You **are** lucky.   You **are** my friend.

Are is also used when there is more than one person or thing.
Blanca and Charley **are** at school.   They **are** in second grade.

Complete It

Read each sentence below. Choose the correct verb from the parentheses ( ). Write it on the line.

1. I ___am___ tall and strong. (is, am)

2. You ___are___ a great cook. (are, am)

3. Gavin and Mitch ___are___ twins. (is, are)

4. This soup ___is___ too spicy! (is, am)

5. I ___am___ a niece. (are, am)

6. All the girls in my class ___are___ excited. (is, are)

7. That skateboard ___is___ broken. (are, is)

84

Lesson 3.3 Irregular Verbs: **Am, Is, Are**

Proof It

Read the diary entry below. The wrong forms of the verbs **am, is,** and **are** are used. Cross out each incorrect verb in bold type. Then, write the correct form above it.

Thursday, May 27

Dear Diary,
    Victoria ~~are~~ [is] my friend. She knows lots of jokes. Today, I told her, "You ~~am~~ [are] the funniest person I know! I ~~are~~ [am] glad to be your friend."
    We ~~is~~ [are] in a club together. Owen and Rachel ~~is~~ [are] in the club, too. We learn all kinds of jokes. Knock-knock jokes ~~is~~ [are] my favorite. Riddles ~~am~~ [are] Victoria's favorite. Owen ~~are~~ [is] older than us. He ~~am~~ [is] in third grade. He tells us all the third-grade jokes. We spend a lot of time laughing!

Try It

1. Write a sentence with only one person or thing. Use **is**.
___Answers will vary.___

2. Write a sentence with more than one person or thing. Use **are**.
___Answers will vary.___

85

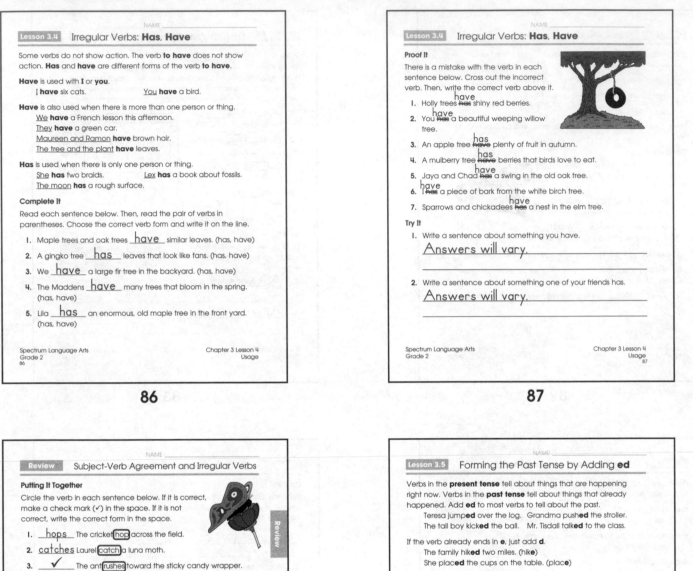

Lesson 3.4 Irregular Verbs: **Has**, **Have**

Some verbs do not show action. The verb **to have** does not show action. **Has** and **have** are different forms of the verb **to have**.

Have is used with **I** or **you**.

I **have** six cats. You **have** a bird.

Have is also used when there is more than one person or thing.
We **have** a French lesson this afternoon.
They **have** a green car.
Maureen and Ramon **have** brown hair.
The tree and the plant **have** leaves.

Has is used when there is only one person or thing.
She **has** two braids. Lex **has** a book about fossils.
The moon **has** a rough surface.

Complete It

Read each sentence below. Then, read the pair of verbs in parentheses. Choose the correct verb form and write it on the line.

1. Maple trees and oak trees __have__ similar leaves. (has, have)

2. A gingko tree __has__ leaves that look like fans. (has, have)

3. We __have__ a large fir tree in the backyard. (has, have)

4. The Maddens __have__ many trees that bloom in the spring. (has, have)

5. Lila __has__ an enormous, old maple tree in the front yard. (has, have)

Spectrum Language Arts
Grade 2
86

Chapter 3 Lesson 4
Usage

86

Lesson 3.4 Irregular Verbs: **Has**, **Have**

Proof It
There is a mistake with the verb in each sentence below. Cross out the incorrect verb. Then, write the correct verb above it.

1. Holly trees ~~has~~ *have* shiny red berries.

2. You ~~has~~ *have* a beautiful weeping willow tree.

3. An apple tree ~~have~~ *has* plenty of fruit in autumn.

4. A mulberry tree ~~have~~ *has* berries that birds love to eat.

5. Jaya and Chad ~~has~~ *have* a swing in the old oak tree.

6. I ~~has~~ *have* a piece of bark from the white birch tree.

7. Sparrows and chickadees ~~has~~ *have* a nest in the elm tree.

Try It

1. Write a sentence about something you have.

   Answers will vary.

2. Write a sentence about something one of your friends has.

   Answers will vary.

Spectrum Language Arts
Grade 2

Chapter 3 Lesson 4
Usage
87

87

Review Subject-Verb Agreement and Irregular Verbs

Putting It Together

Circle the verb in each sentence below. If it is correct, make a check mark (✓) in the space. If it is not correct, write the correct form in the space.

1. __hops__ The cricket (hop) across the field.

2. __catches__ Laurel (catch) a luna moth.

3. __✓__ The ant (rushes) toward the sticky candy wrapper.

4. __land__ The ladybugs (lands) on the porch.

5. __watch__ The twins (watches) the praying mantis under the tree.

6. __✓__ The lightning bug (flashes) in the sky.

Read each sentence below. Then, read the pair of verbs in parentheses ( ). Choose the correct verb form, and write it in the space.

1. Zach and Grace __have__ a butterfly garden. (have, has)

2. The grasshopper and the beetle __are__ green. (is, are)

3. The inchworm __is__ under the large rock. (am, is)

4. I __am__ lucky that the dragonfly landed on my arm. (am, are)

5. The fly __has__ two wings. (have, has)

Spectrum Language Arts
Grade 2

Review: Chapter 3 Lessons 1–4
Usage
89

89

Lesson 3.5 Forming the Past Tense by Adding **ed**

Verbs in the **present tense** tell about things that are happening right now. Verbs in the **past tense** tell about things that already happened. Add **ed** to most verbs to tell about the past.
Teresa jump**ed** over the log. Grandma push**ed** the stroller.
The tall boy kick**ed** the ball. Mr. Tisdall talk**ed** to the class.

If the verb already ends in **e**, just add **d**.
The family hik**ed** two miles. (hike)
She plac**ed** the cups on the table. (place)

Complete It

The sentences below are missing verbs. Complete each sentence with the past tense of the verb in parentheses ( ).

1. Annie Smith Peck __traveled__ to many countries. (travel)

2. In 1888, she __climbed__ Mount Shasta in California. (climb)

3. She __hoped__ to climb the Matterhorn one day. (hope)

4. Annie __started__ a group called the American Alpine Club. (start)

5. She __explored__ the volcanoes of South America. (explore)

6. She __worked__ hard so she could climb in her spare time. (work)

7. Annie __continued__ climbing until she was 82. (continue)

Spectrum Language Arts
Grade 2
90

Chapter 3 Lesson 5
Usage

90

Answer Key

Lesson 3.5   Forming the Past Tense by Adding **ed**

Rewrite It

Rewrite the sentences below in the past tense by adding **ed** to the underlined verb. If the verb already ends in **e**, just add **d** to change it to the past tense.

Example: Darby <u>pull</u> on his leash. Darby **pulled** on his leash.

1. Annie Smith Peck <u>climb</u> many mountains.

Annie Smith Peck climbed many mountains.

2. She <u>live</u> from 1850 until 1935.

She lived from 1850 until 1935.

3. Annie <u>show</u> the world how strong women can be.

Annie showed the world how strong women can be.

4. She <u>want</u> to set records in climbing.

She wanted to set records in climbing.

Try It

Write two sentences about what you did last week. Make sure the verbs are in the past tense.

1. _____

2. _____

Answers will vary but should be written in the past tense.

Spectrum Language Arts
Grade 2

Chapter 3 Lesson 5
Usage
91

91

Lesson 3.6   Past-Tense Verbs: **Was, Were**

The past tense of **am** and **is** is **was**. Remember to use was only if there is one person or thing.

    I **was** tired.   The house **was** white.

The past tense of **are** is **were**. Remember to use **were** if there is more than one person or thing.

    We **were** a team.   The monkeys **were** funny.

Complete It

Write the correct past-tense verb in the blanks below. Use **was** or **were**.

Last Tuesday, my brother Benjamin __was__ on TV. He __was__ at the park with his friend Allison. It __was__ a sunny day. They __were__ on the jungle gym. A news reporter __was__ at the park, too. She __was__ a reporter for Channel WBVA news. She asked people in the park if the city should build a new pool. Benjamin and Allison __were__ excited about the interview. My family watched Benjamin on the evening news. I __was__ proud of my brother, the TV star!

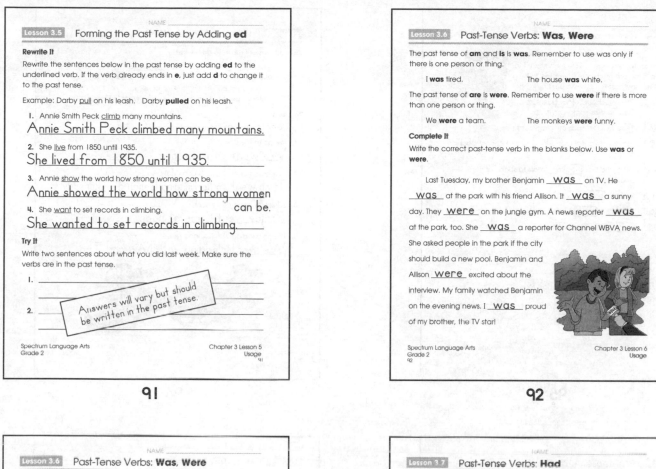

Spectrum Language Arts
Grade 2
92

Chapter 3 Lesson 6
Usage

92

Lesson 3.6   Past-Tense Verbs: **Was, Were**

Rewrite It

The sentences below are in the present tense. Rewrite them in the past tense.

Example: The basketball <u>is</u> in the gym. The basketball was in the gym.

1. Benjamin <u>is</u> worried we would miss the news.

Benjamin was worried we would miss the news.

2. Mom and Dad <u>are</u> happy to see Ben's good manners.

Mom and Dad were happy to see Ben's good manners.

3. I <u>am</u> glad Ben wore the hat I gave him.

I was glad Ben wore the hat I gave him.

4. You <u>are</u> on vacation.

You were on vacation.

Try It

1. Write a sentence about something that is happening right now. Use the verb **is** in your sentence.

Answers will vary.

2. Now, write the same sentence in the past tense.

Answers will vary.

Spectrum Language Arts
Grade 2

Chapter 3 Lesson 6
Usage
93

93

Lesson 3.7   Past-Tense Verbs: **Had**

The past tense of **have** and **has** is **had**

Present Tense	Past Tense
I **have** four pets.	I **had** four pets.
The flowers **have** red petals.	The flowers **had** red petals.
Hayden **has** short hair.	Hayden **had** short hair.

Complete It

Complete each sentence with the correct form of the verb **have**. The word in parentheses ( ) will tell you to use the present tense or the past tense.

1. My bike __has__ a horn and a scoop seat. (present)

2. My mom __had__ a bike just like it when she was little. (past)

3. The wheels __have__ shiny silver spokes. (present)

4. My mom's old bike __had__ a bell, too. (past)

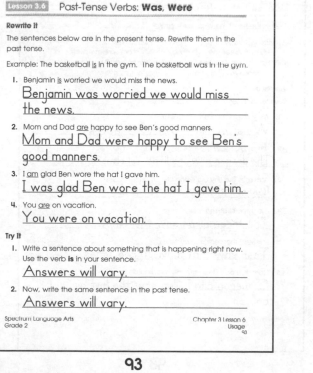

Spectrum Language Arts
Grade 2
94

Chapter 3 Lesson 7
Usage

94

Lesson 3.7 Past-Tense Verbs: **Had**

Identify It

Read each sentence below. Circle the verb. If the sentence is in the present tense, write **pres.** in the space. If it is in the past tense, write **past**.

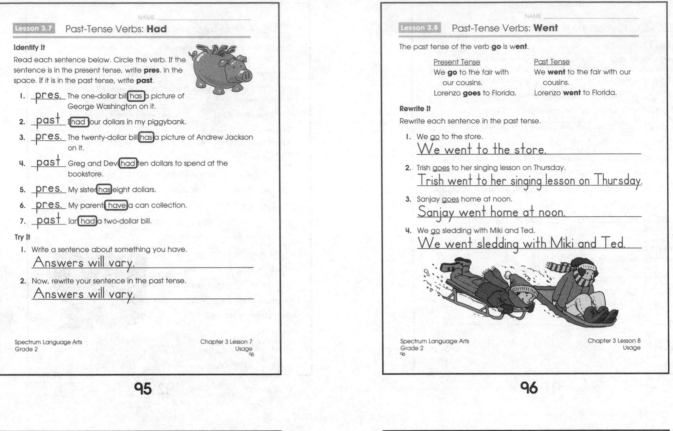

1. **pres.** The one-dollar bill (has) a picture of George Washington on it.
2. **past** I (had) four dollars in my piggybank.
3. **pres.** The twenty-dollar bill (has) a picture of Andrew Jackson on it.
4. **past** Greg and Devi (had) ten dollars to spend at the bookstore.
5. **pres.** My sister (has) eight dollars.
6. **pres.** My parents (have) a can collection.
7. **past** Ian (had) a two-dollar bill.

Try It

1. Write a sentence about something you have.
   Answers will vary.

2. Now, rewrite your sentence in the past tense.
   Answers will vary.

Spectrum Language Arts
Grade 2
Chapter 3 Lesson 7
Usage
95

95

Lesson 3.8 Past-Tense Verbs: **Went**

The past tense of the verb **go** is w**ent**.

Present Tense	Past Tense
We **go** to the fair with our cousins.	We **went** to the fair with our cousins.
Lorenzo **goes** to Florida.	Lorenzo **went** to Florida.

Rewrite It

Rewrite each sentence in the past tense.

1. We <u>go</u> to the store.
   We went to the store.

2. Trish <u>goes</u> to her singing lesson on Thursday.
   Trish went to her singing lesson on Thursday.

3. Sanjay <u>goes</u> home at noon.
   Sanjay went home at noon.

4. We <u>go</u> sledding with Miki and Ted.
   We went sledding with Miki and Ted.

Spectrum Language Arts
Grade 2
96
Chapter 3 Lesson 8
Usage

96

Lesson 3.8 Past-Tense Verbs: **Went**

Proof It

Some of the verbs below are in the wrong tense. Cross out the underlined verbs. Write the correct past-tense verbs above them.

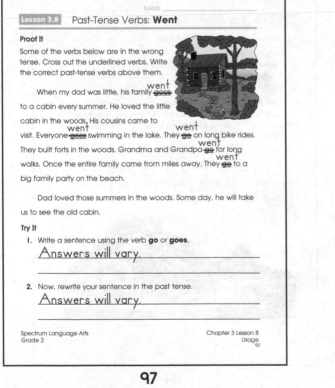

When my dad was little, his family ~~goes~~ *went* to a cabin every summer. He loved the little cabin in the woods. His cousins came to visit. Everyone ~~goes~~ *went* swimming in the lake. They ~~go~~ *went* on long bike rides. They built forts in the woods. Grandma and Grandpa ~~go~~ *went* for long walks. Once the entire family came from miles away. They ~~go~~ *went* to a big family party on the beach.

Dad loved those summers in the woods. Some day, he will take us to see the old cabin.

Try It

1. Write a sentence using the verb **go** or **goes**.
   Answers will vary.

2. Now, rewrite your sentence in the past tense.
   Answers will vary.

Spectrum Language Arts
Grade 2
Chapter 3 Lesson 8
Usage
97

97

Lesson 3.9 Past-Tense Verbs: **Saw**

The past tense of the verb **see** is **saw**.

Present Tense	Past Tense
My mom **sees** me swimming.	My mom **saw** me swimming.
Franco and Ana **see** the puppy every day.	Franco and Ana **saw** the puppy every day.

Rewrite It

Rewrite each sentence in the past tense.

1. We <u>see</u> raindrops on the leaves.
   We saw raindrops on the leaves.

2. The dragon <u>sees</u> the little girl climbing the hill.
   The dragon saw the little girl climbing the hill.

3. Dad <u>sees</u> the tiny cut when he put on his glasses.
   Dad saw the tiny cut when he put on his glasses.

4. The three birds <u>see</u> their mother.
   The three birds saw their mother.

5. Tess <u>sees</u> that movie three times.
   Tess saw that movie three times.

6. Cameron and Dillon <u>see</u> the hot air balloon.
   Cameron and Dillon saw the hot air balloon.

Spectrum Language Arts
Grade 2
98
Chapter 3 Lesson 9
Usage

98

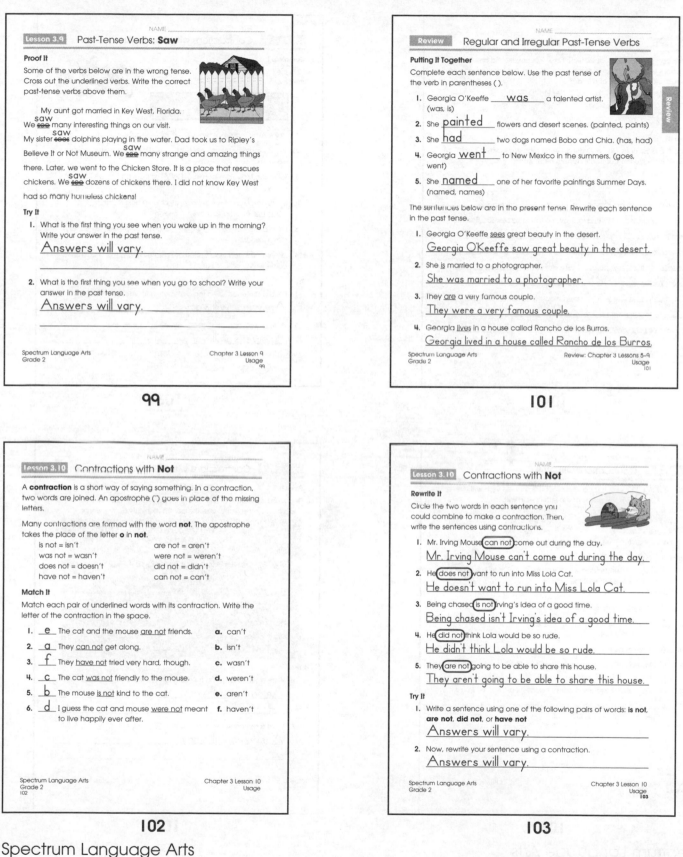

Lesson 3.9 Past-Tense Verbs: **Saw**

Proof It

Some of the verbs below are in the wrong tense. Cross out the underlined verbs. Write the correct past-tense verbs above them.

My aunt got married in Key West, Florida.
We ~~see~~ **saw** many interesting things on our visit.
My sister ~~sees~~ **saw** dolphins playing in the water. Dad took us to Ripley's Believe It or Not Museum. We ~~see~~ **saw** many strange and amazing things there. Later, we went to the Chicken Store. It is a place that rescues chickens. We ~~see~~ **saw** dozens of chickens there. I did not know Key West had so many homeless chickens!

Try It

1. What is the first thing you see when you wake up in the morning? Write your answer in the past tense.

   Answers will vary.

2. What is the first thing you see when you go to school? Write your answer in the past tense.

   Answers will vary.

Spectrum Language Arts
Grade 2

Chapter 3 Lesson 9
Usage
99

99

Putting It Together

Complete each sentence below. Use the past tense of the verb in parentheses ( ).

1. Georgia O'Keeffe **was** a talented artist. (was, is)

2. She **painted** flowers and desert scenes. (painted, paints)

3. She **had** two dogs named Bobo and Chia. (has, had)

4. Georgia **went** to New Mexico in the summers. (goes, went)

5. She **named** one of her favorite paintings Summer Days. (named, names)

The sentences below are in the present tense. Rewrite each sentence in the past tense.

1. Georgia O'Keeffe <u>sees</u> great beauty in the desert.

   Georgia O'Keeffe saw great beauty in the desert.

2. She <u>is</u> married to a photographer.

   She was married to a photographer.

3. They <u>are</u> a very famous couple.

   They were a very famous couple.

4. Georgia <u>lives</u> in a house called Rancho de los Burros.

   Georgia lived in a house called Rancho de los Burros.

Spectrum Language Arts
Grade 2

Review: Chapter 3 Lessons 5–9
Usage
101

101

Lesson 3.10 Contractions with **Not**

A **contraction** is a short way of saying something. In a contraction, two words are joined. An apostrophe (') goes in place of the missing letters.

Many contractions are formed with the word **not**. The apostrophe takes the place of the letter **o** in **not**.

is not = isn't	are not = aren't
was not = wasn't	were not = weren't
does not = doesn't	did not = didn't
have not = haven't	can not = can't

Match It

Match each pair of underlined words with its contraction. Write the letter of the contraction in the space.

1. **e** The cat and the mouse <u>are not</u> friends.   **a.** can't
2. **a** They <u>can not</u> get along.   **b.** isn't
3. **f** They <u>have not</u> tried very hard, though.   **c.** wasn't
4. **c** The cat <u>was not</u> friendly to the mouse.   **d.** weren't
5. **b** The mouse <u>is not</u> kind to the cat.   **e.** aren't
6. **d** I guess the cat and mouse <u>were not</u> meant to live happily ever after.   **f.** haven't

Spectrum Language Arts
Grade 2
102

Chapter 3 Lesson 10
Usage

102

Lesson 3.10 Contractions with **Not**

Rewrite It

Circle the two words in each sentence you could combine to make a contraction. Then, write the sentences using contractions.

1. Mr. Irving Mouse (can not) come out during the day.

   Mr. Irving Mouse can't come out during the day.

2. He (does not) want to run into Miss Lola Cat.

   He doesn't want to run into Miss Lola Cat.

3. Being chased (is not) Irving's idea of a good time.

   Being chased isn't Irving's idea of a good time.

4. He (did not) think Lola would be so rude.

   He didn't think Lola would be so rude.

5. They (are not) going to be able to share this house.

   They aren't going to be able to share this house.

Try It

1. Write a sentence using one of the following pairs of words: **is not**, **are not**, **did not**, or **have not**

   Answers will vary.

2. Now, rewrite your sentence using a contraction.

   Answers will vary.

Spectrum Language Arts
Grade 2

Chapter 3 Lesson 10
Usage
103

103

Answer Key

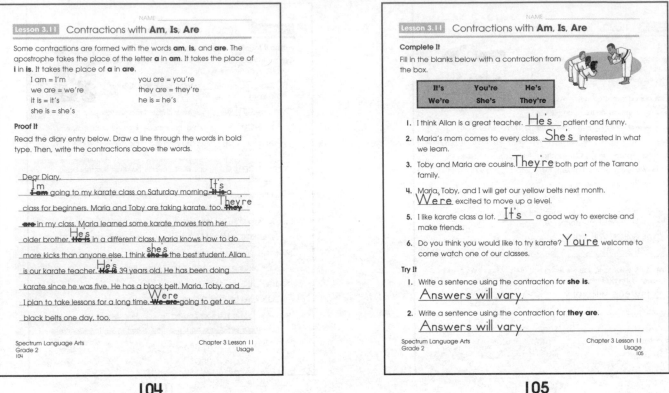

NAME

Lesson 3.11 Contractions with **Am**, **Is**, **Are**

Some contractions are formed with the words **am**, **is**, and **are**. The apostrophe takes the place of the letter **a** in **am**. It takes the place of **i** in **is**. It takes the place of **a** in **are**.

I am = I'm
we are = we're
it is = it's
she is = she's

you are = you're
they are = they're
he is = he's

Proof It

Read the diary entry below. Draw a line through the words in bold type. Then, write the contractions above the words.

Dear Diary,

I'm
~~I am~~ going to my karate class on Saturday morning. **It's** ~~It is~~ a
class for beginners. Maria and Toby are taking karate, too. **They're** ~~They are~~ in my class. Maria learned some karate moves from her
He's
older brother. ~~He is~~ in a different class. Maria knows how to do
she's
more kicks than anyone else. I think ~~she is~~ the best student. Allan
He's
is our karate teacher. ~~He is~~ 39 years old. He has been doing
karate since he was five. He has a black belt. Maria, Toby, and
We're
I plan to take lessons for a long time. ~~We are~~ going to get our
black belts one day, too.

Spectrum Language Arts
Grade 2
104

Chapter 3 Lesson 11
Usage

104

NAME

Lesson 3.11 Contractions with **Am**, **Is**, **Are**

Complete It

Fill in the blanks below with a contraction from the box.

It's	You're	He's
We're	She's	They're

1. I think Allan is a great teacher. **He's** patient and funny.

2. Maria's mom comes to every class. **She's** interested in what we learn.

3. Toby and Maria are cousins. **They're** both part of the Tarrano family.

4. Maria, Toby, and I will get our yellow belts next month. **We're** excited to move up a level.

5. I like karate class a lot. **It's** a good way to exercise and make friends.

6. Do you think you would like to try karate? **You're** welcome to come watch one of our classes.

Try It

1. Write a sentence using the contraction for **she is**.
   Answers will vary.

2. Write a sentence using the contraction for **they are**.
   Answers will vary.

Spectrum Language Arts
Grade 2

Chapter 3 Lesson 11
Usage
105

105

NAME

Lesson 3.12 Contractions with **Will**

Many contractions are formed with pronouns and the verb **will**. An apostrophe (') takes the place of the letters **wi** in **will**.

I will = I'll
you will = you'll
she will = she'll
he will = he'll

it will = it'll
we will = we'll
they will = they'll

Match It

Match each pair of underlined words with its contraction. Write the letter of the contraction in the space.

1. **c** I will travel into space one day.
2. **f** A spaceship will take me there. It will move very fast.
3. **e** You will be my co-pilot.
4. **a** My sister, Eva, can come along, too. She will direct the spaceship.
5. **b** We will make many important discoveries.
6. **d** Our families can have a party when we return. They will be so proud!

a. She'll
b. We'll
c. I'll
d. They'll
e. You'll
f. It'll

Spectrum Language Arts
Grade 2
106

Chapter 3 Lesson 12
Usage

106

NAME

Lesson 3.12 Contractions with **Will**

Proof It

Read the newspaper article below. Draw a line through the underlined words. Then, write the contractions above the words.

Hughes to Become Youngest Astronaut

Jasmine Hughes is only nine years old. **She'll** ~~She will~~ be the first child to journey into space. Jasmine has been training since she was four. **She'll** ~~She will~~ travel on the space shuttle Investigator. Six other astronauts will be in her crew. **They'll** ~~They will~~ have to work well as a team. Darren Unger will be the commander. **He'll** ~~He will~~ be the leader of the crew. They know their mission is important. **It'll** ~~It will~~ help scientists learn more about the universe. The world will be able to watch parts of the trip on TV. **We'll** ~~We will~~ see history being made!

Try It

1. Write a sentence using the contraction for **he will**.
   Answers will vary.

2. Write a sentence using the contraction for **I will**.
   Answers will vary.

Spectrum Language Arts
Grade 2

Chapter 3 Lesson 12
Usage
107

107

Spectrum Language Arts
Grade 2

Answer Key

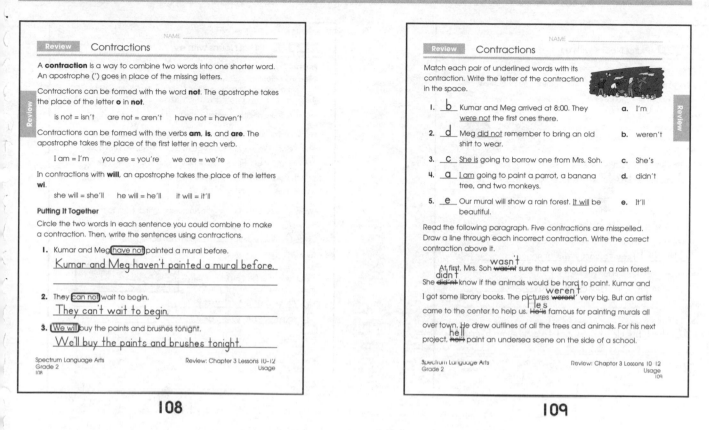

Page 108

Review Contractions

A **contraction** is a way to combine two words into one shorter word. An apostrophe (') goes in place of the missing letters.

Contractions can be formed with the word **not**. The apostrophe takes the place of the letter **o** in **not**.

is not = isn't   are not = aren't   have not = haven't

Contractions can be formed with the verbs **am**, **is**, and **are**. The apostrophe takes the place of the first letter in each verb.

I am = I'm   you are = you're   we are = we're

In contractions with **will**, an apostrophe takes the place of the letters **wi**.

she will = she'll   he will = he'll   it will = it'll

Putting It Together

Circle the two words in each sentence you could combine to make a contraction. Then, write the sentences using contractions.

1. Kumar and Meg (have not) painted a mural before.

   Kumar and Meg haven't painted a mural before.

2. They (can not) wait to begin.

   They can't wait to begin.

3. (We will) buy the paints and brushes tonight.

   We'll buy the paints and brushes tonight.

Spectrum Language Arts
Grade 2
108
Review: Chapter 3 Lessons 10-12
Usage

Page 109

Review Contractions

Match each pair of underlined words with its contraction. Write the letter of the contraction in the space.

1. _b_ Kumar and Meg arrived at 8:00. They <u>were not</u> the first ones there.   a. I'm

2. _d_ Meg <u>did not</u> remember to bring an old shirt to wear.   b. weren't

3. _c_ <u>She is</u> going to borrow one from Mrs. Soh.   c. She's

4. _a_ <u>I am</u> going to paint a parrot, a banana tree, and two monkeys.   d. didn't

5. _e_ Our mural will show a rain forest. <u>It will</u> be beautiful.   e. It'll

Read the following paragraph. Five contractions are misspelled. Draw a line through each incorrect contraction. Write the correct contraction above it.

At first, Mrs. Soh ~~was'nt~~ wasn't sure that we should paint a rain forest. She ~~did'nt~~ didn't know if the animals would be hard to paint. Kumar and I got some library books. The pictures ~~were'nt~~ weren't very big. But an artist came to the center to help us. ~~He is~~ He's famous for painting murals all over town. He drew outlines of all the trees and animals. For his next project, ~~he'l~~ he'll paint an undersea scene on the side of a school.

Spectrum Language Arts
Grade 2
Review: Chapter 3 Lessons 10-12
Usage
109

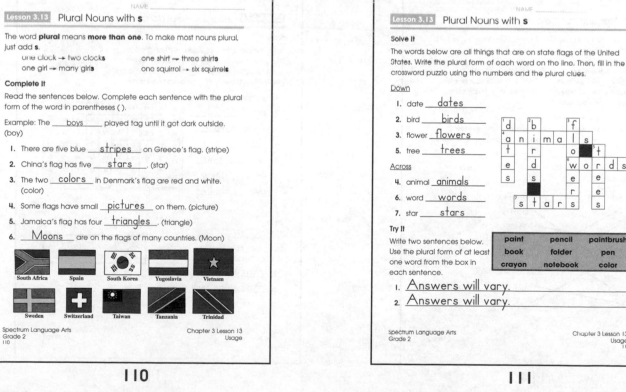

Page 110

Lesson 3.13 Plural Nouns with **s**

The word **plural** means **more than one**. To make most nouns plural, just add **s**.

one clock → two clock**s**   one shirt → three shirt**s**
one girl → many girl**s**   one squirrel → six squirrel**s**

Complete It

Read the sentences below. Complete each sentence with the plural form of the word in parentheses ( ).

Example: The ___boys___ played tag until it got dark outside. (boy)

1. There are five blue ___stripes___ on Greece's flag. (stripe)
2. China's flag has five ___stars___. (star)
3. The two ___colors___ in Denmark's flag are red and white. (color)
4. Some flags have small ___pictures___ on them. (picture)
5. Jamaica's flag has four ___triangles___. (triangle)
6. ___Moons___ are on the flags of many countries. (Moon)

South Africa   Spain   South Korea   Yugoslavia   Vietnam
Sweden   Switzerland   Taiwan   Tanzania   Trinidad

Spectrum Language Arts
Grade 2
110
Chapter 3 Lesson 13
Usage

Page 111

Lesson 3.13 Plural Nouns with **s**

Solve It

The words below are all things that are on state flags of the United States. Write the plural form of each word on the line. Then, fill in the crossword puzzle using the numbers and the plural clues.

Down
1. date ___dates___
2. bird ___birds___
3. flower ___flowers___
5. tree ___trees___

Across
4. animal ___animals___
6. word ___words___
7. star ___stars___

Try It

Write two sentences below. Use the plural form of at least one word from the box in each sentence.

paint   pencil   paintbrush
book   folder   pen
crayon   notebook   color

1. Answers will vary.
2. Answers will vary.

Spectrum Language Arts
Grade 2
Chapter 3 Lesson 13
Usage
111

Answer Key

Lesson 3.14 Plural Nouns with **es**

If a noun ends in **sh**, **ch**, **s**, or **x**, add **es** to make it plural.

one ax → two ax**es**   one brush → many brush**es**

one pouch → six pouch**es**   one bus → seven bus**es**

Rewrite It

Read the sentences below. Then, write the sentences with the plural form of the underlined words.

1. There are two <u>bunch</u> of grapes on the table.
   There are two bunches of grapes on the table.

2. The <u>peach</u> are in the basket.
   The peaches are in the basket.

3. Use the <u>box</u> to carry the oranges.
   Use the boxes to carry the oranges.

4. Please put the fruit in the yellow <u>dish</u>.
   Please put the fruit in the yellow dishes.

5. Each of the <u>class</u> will get to pick some berries.
   Each of the classes will get to pick some berries.

Spectrum Language Arts
Grade 2
112

Chapter 3 Lesson 14
Usage

112

Lesson 3.14 Plural Nouns with **es**

Proof It

Read the paragraphs below. The underlined words should be plural. To make a word plural, make a caret (^) at the end of the word. Then, write the letter or letters you want to add above the caret.

Example: There are three **watch**^es in the glass case.

We waited on the <u>bench</u>^es outside the school. The <u>bus</u>^es picked us up at nine o'clock. We went to Sunnyvale Apple Orchard. Mr. Krup gave us some <u>box</u>^es to use. He showed us how to pick ripe apples. Many <u>branch</u>^es were heavy with fruit. There were also some blueberry <u>bush</u>^es on the farm.

When we were done picking, the tractor brought us back to the farmhouse. We ate our <u>lunch</u>^es at some picnic tables. Mrs. Krup gave us <u>glass</u>^es of lemonade. Tomorrow, we'll make apple pies.

Try It

Write two sentences below. Use the plural form of at least one word from the box in each sentence.

fox	watch
beach	brush

1. Answers will vary.
2. Answers will vary.

Spectrum Language Arts
Grade 2

Chapter 3 Lesson 14
Usage
113

113

Lesson 3.15 Irregular Plural Nouns

Some plural nouns do not follow the rules you have learned. To form the plurals of these nouns, do not add **s** or **es**. Instead, the whole word changes. Here are some examples.

one **man** → three **men**   one **foot** → two **feet**
one **woman** → eight **women**   one **goose** → four **geese**
one **child** → a few **children** one **tooth** → many **teeth**
one **mouse** → twenty **mice**

Some nouns do not change at all in their plural forms.

one **deer** → many **deer**   one **moose** → nine **moose**
one **fish** → sixty **fish**   one **sheep** → one hundred **sheep**

Match It

Read the phrases in Column 1. Then, draw a line to match each phrase to its plural in Column 2.

Column 1   Column 2
one tooth   nine deer
one child   four feet
one foot   twelve mice
one goose   several teeth
one deer   lots of children
one mouse   two men
one man   seven geese

Spectrum Language Arts
Grade 2
114

Chapter 3 Lesson 15
Usage

114

Lesson 3.15 Irregular Plural Nouns

Solve It

Write the plural form of each word on the line. Then, see if you can find each plural word in the word search puzzle. Circle the words you find in the puzzle. Words can be found across and down.

1. woman ___women___
2. fish ___fish___
3. moose ___moose___
4. mouse ___mice___
5. foot ___feet___
6. sheep ___sheep___
7. child ___children___
8. tooth ___teeth___

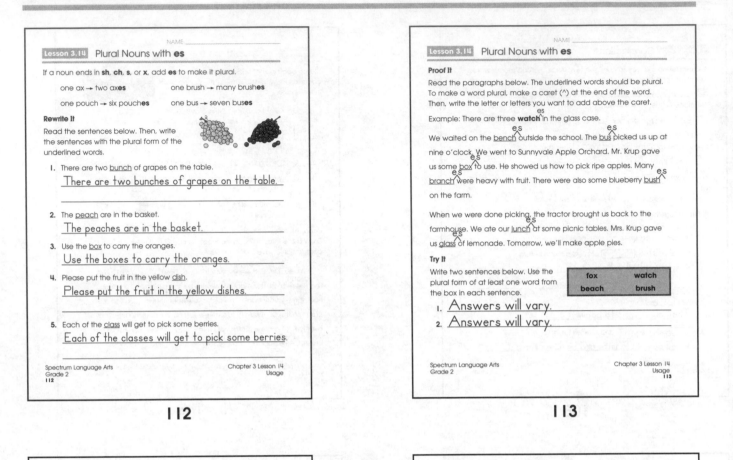

n	l	m	i	h	l	f	g	c	q
c	h	i	l	d	r	e	n	b	u
n	t	c	t	l	w	e	i	h	x
s	h	e	e	p	o	t	v	k	m
f	s	a	e	k	m	o	o	s	e
e	r	h	t	g	e	d	f	z	p
f	i	s	h	j	n	p	u	g	j

Try It

Write two sentences below. Use the plural form of at least one word from the box in each sentence.

foot	mouse
man	deer
fish	goose

1. Answers will vary.
2. Answers will vary.

Spectrum Language Arts
Grade 2

Chapter 3 Lesson 15
Usage
115

115

Spectrum Language Arts
Grade 2

Answer Key

Answer Key

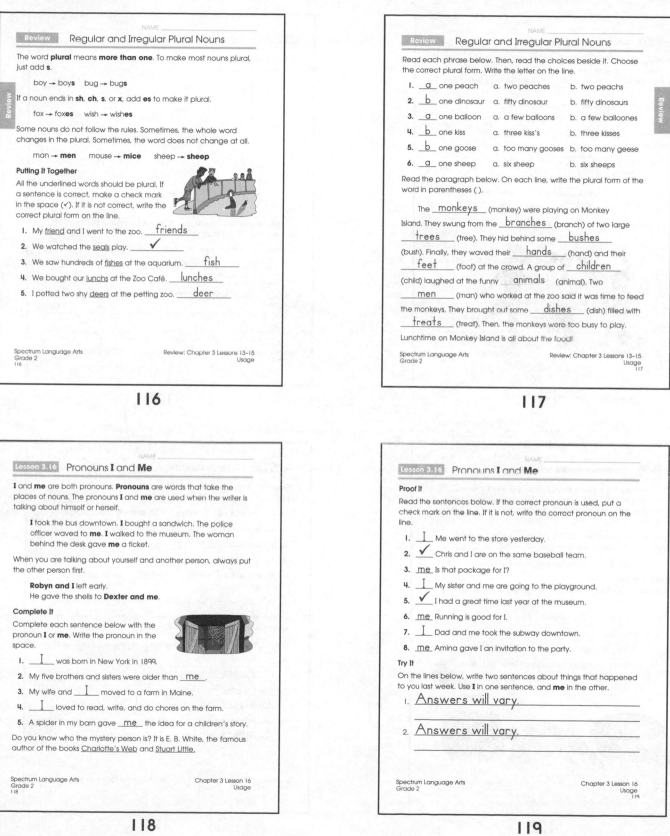

Review   Regular and Irregular Plural Nouns

The word **plural** means **more than one**. To make most nouns plural, just add **s**.

     boy → boy**s**   bug → bug**s**

If a noun ends in **sh**, **ch**, **s**, or **x**, add **es** to make it plural.

     fox → fox**es**   wish → wish**es**

Some nouns do not follow the rules. Sometimes, the whole word changes in the plural. Sometimes, the word does not change at all.

     man → **men**   mouse → **mice**   sheep → **sheep**

Putting It Together

All the underlined words should be plural. If a sentence is correct, make a check mark in the space (✓). If it is not correct, write the correct plural form on the line.

1. My <u>friend</u> and I went to the zoo. __friends__
2. We watched the <u>seals</u> play. __✓__
3. We saw hundreds of <u>fishes</u> at the aquarium. __fish__
4. We bought our <u>lunchs</u> at the Zoo Café. __lunches__
5. I petted two shy <u>deers</u> at the petting zoo. __deer__

Spectrum Language Arts
Grade 2
116

Review: Chapter 3 Lessons 13–15
Usage

116

Review   Regular and Irregular Plural Nouns

Read each phrase below. Then, read the choices beside it. Choose the correct plural form. Write the letter on the line.

1. __a__ one peach   a. two peaches   b. two peachs
2. __b__ one dinosaur   a. fifty dinosaur   b. fifty dinosaurs
3. __a__ one balloon   a. a few balloons   b. a few balloones
4. __b__ one kiss   a. three kiss's   b. three kisses
5. __b__ one goose   a. too many gooses   b. too many geese
6. __a__ one sheep   a. six sheep   b. six sheeps

Read the paragraph below. On each line, write the plural form of the word in parentheses ( ).

The __monkeys__ (monkey) were playing on Monkey Island. They swung from the __branches__ (branch) of two large __trees__ (tree). They hid behind some __bushes__ (bush). Finally, they waved their __hands__ (hand) and their __feet__ (foot) at the crowd. A group of __children__ (child) laughed at the funny __animals__ (animal). Two __men__ (man) who worked at the zoo said it was time to feed the monkeys. They brought out some __dishes__ (dish) filled with __treats__ (treat). Then, the monkeys were too busy to play. Lunchtime on Monkey Island is all about the food!

Lesson 3.16   Pronouns **I** and **Me**

I and **me** are both pronouns. **Pronouns** are words that take the places of nouns. The pronouns **I** and **me** are used when the writer is talking about himself or herself.

> **I** took the bus downtown. **I** bought a sandwich. The police officer waved to **me**. **I** walked to the museum. The woman behind the desk gave **me** a ticket.

When you are talking about yourself and another person, always put the other person first.

> **Robyn and I** left early.
> He gave the shells to **Dexter and me**.

Complete It

Complete each sentence below with the pronoun **I** or **me**. Write the pronoun in the space.

1. __I__ was born in New York in 1899.
2. My five brothers and sisters were older than __me__.
3. My wife and __I__ moved to a farm in Maine.
4. __I__ loved to read, write, and do chores on the farm.
5. A spider in my barn gave __me__ the idea for a children's story.

Do you know who the mystery person is? It is E. B. White, the famous author of the books <u>Charlotte's Web</u> and <u>Stuart Little</u>.

Spectrum Language Arts
Grade 2
118

Chapter 3 Lesson 16
Usage

118

Lesson 3.16   Pronouns **I** and **Me**

Proof It

Read the sentences below. If the correct pronoun is used, put a check mark on the line. If it is not, write the correct pronoun on the line.

1. __I__ Me went to the store yesterday.
2. __✓__ Chris and I are on the same baseball team.
3. __me__ Is that package for I?
4. __I__ My sister and me are going to the playground.
5. __✓__ I had a great time last year at the museum.
6. __me__ Running is good for I.
7. __I__ Dad and me took the subway downtown.
8. __me__ Amina gave I an invitation to the party.

Try It

On the lines below, write two sentences about things that happened to you last week. Use **I** in one sentence, and **me** in the other.

1. __Answers will vary.__

2. __Answers will vary.__

Spectrum Language Arts
Grade 2

Answer Key
171

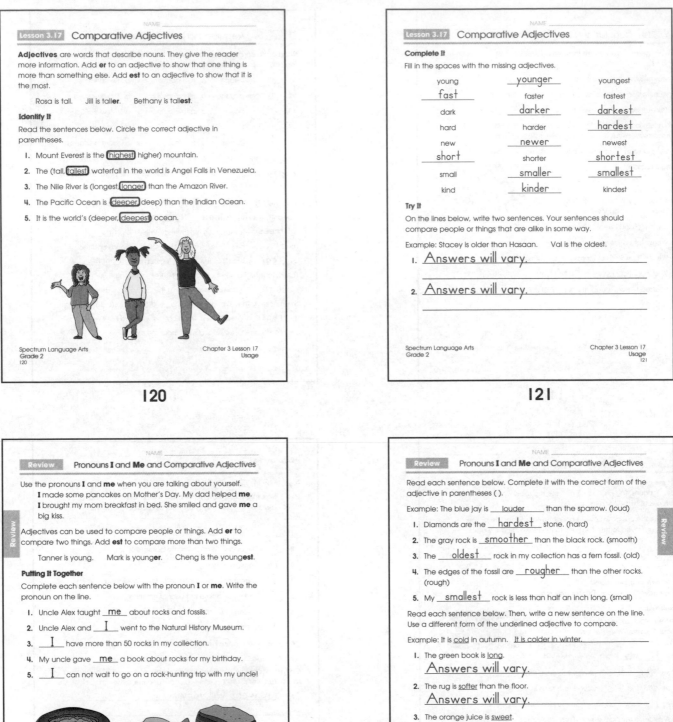

Lesson 3.17 Comparative Adjectives

Adjectives are words that describe nouns. They give the reader more information. Add **er** to an adjective to show that one thing is more than something else. Add **est** to an adjective to show that it is the most.

Rosa is tall.   Jill is tall**er**.   Bethany is tall**est**.

Identify It

Read the sentences below. Circle the correct adjective in parentheses.

1. Mount Everest is the (highest, higher) mountain.
2. The (tall, tallest) waterfall in the world is Angel Falls in Venezuela.
3. The Nile River is (longest, longer) than the Amazon River.
4. The Pacific Ocean is (deeper, deep) than the Indian Ocean.
5. It is the world's (deeper, deepest) ocean.

Spectrum Language Arts
Grade 2
120

Chapter 3 Lesson 17
Usage

120

Lesson 3.17 Comparative Adjectives

Complete It

Fill in the spaces with the missing adjectives.

young	younger	youngest
fast	faster	fastest
dark	darker	darkest
hard	harder	hardest
new	newer	newest
short	shorter	shortest
small	smaller	smallest
kind	kinder	kindest

Try It

On the lines below, write two sentences. Your sentences should compare people or things that are alike in some way.

Example: Stacey is older than Hasaan.   Val is the oldest.

1. Answers will vary.

2. Answers will vary.

Spectrum Language Arts
Grade 2

Chapter 3 Lesson 17
Usage
121

121

Review Pronouns **I** and **Me** and Comparative Adjectives

Use the pronouns **I** and **me** when you are talking about yourself.
   I made some pancakes on Mother's Day. My dad helped **me**.
   I brought my mom breakfast in bed. She smiled and gave **me** a big kiss.

Adjectives can be used to compare people or things. Add **er** to compare two things. Add **est** to compare more than two things.

Tanner is young.   Mark is young**er**.   Cheng is the young**est**.

Putting It Together

Complete each sentence below with the pronoun **I** or **me**. Write the pronoun on the line.

1. Uncle Alex taught **me** about rocks and fossils.
2. Uncle Alex and **I** went to the Natural History Museum.
3. **I** have more than 50 rocks in my collection.
4. My uncle gave **me** a book about rocks for my birthday.
5. **I** can not wait to go on a rock-hunting trip with my uncle!

Spectrum Language Arts
Grade 2
122

Review: Chapter 3 Lessons 16-17
Usage

122

Review Pronouns **I** and **Me** and Comparative Adjectives

Read each sentence below. Complete it with the correct form of the adjective in parentheses ( ).

Example: The blue jay is ___louder___ than the sparrow. (loud)

1. Diamonds are the ___hardest___ stone. (hard)
2. The gray rock is ___smoother___ than the black rock. (smooth)
3. The ___oldest___ rock in my collection has a fern fossil. (old)
4. The edges of the fossil are ___rougher___ than the other rocks. (rough)
5. My ___smallest___ rock is less than half an inch long. (small)

Read each sentence below. Then, write a new sentence on the line. Use a different form of the underlined adjective to compare.

Example: It is cold in autumn. It is colder in winter.

1. The green book is long.
   Answers will vary.
2. The rug is softer than the floor.
   Answers will vary.
3. The orange juice is sweet.
   Answers will vary.

Spectrum Language Arts
Grade 2

Review: Chapter 3 Lessons 16-17
Usage
123

123

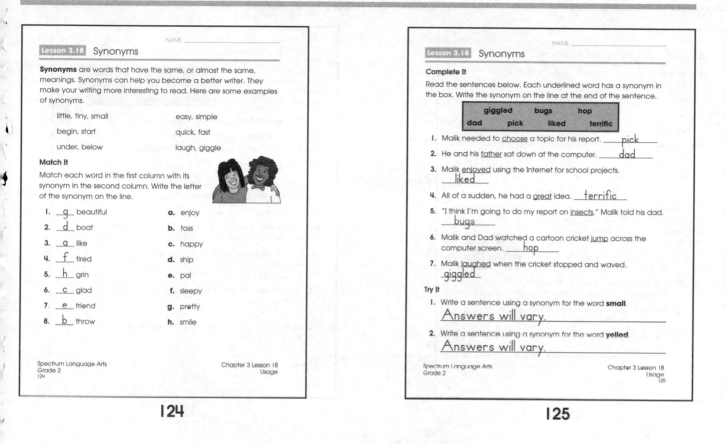

Lesson 3.18 Synonyms

NAME _____

Synonyms are words that have the same, or almost the same, meanings. Synonyms can help you become a better writer. They make your writing more interesting to read. Here are some examples of synonyms.

little, tiny, small	easy, simple
begin, start	quick, fast
under, below	laugh, giggle

Match It

Match each word in the first column with its synonym in the second column. Write the letter of the synonym on the line.

1. _g_ beautiful   **a.** enjoy
2. _d_ boat   **b.** toss
3. _a_ like   **c.** happy
4. _f_ tired   **d.** ship
5. _h_ grin   **e.** pal
6. _c_ glad   **f.** sleepy
7. _e_ friend   **g.** pretty
8. _b_ throw   **h.** smile

Spectrum Language Arts
Grade 2
124

Chapter 3 Lesson 18
Usage

124

Lesson 3.18 Synonyms

NAME _____

Complete It

Read the sentences below. Each underlined word has a synonym in the box. Write the synonym on the line at the end of the sentence.

giggled	bugs	hop
dad	pick	liked	terrific

1. Malik needed to <u>choose</u> a topic for his report. ____pick____
2. He and his <u>father</u> sat down at the computer. ____dad____
3. Malik <u>enjoyed</u> using the Internet for school projects. __liked__
4. All of a sudden, he had a <u>great</u> idea. __terrific__
5. "I think I'm going to do my report on <u>insects</u>," Malik told his dad. __bugs__
6. Malik and Dad watched a cartoon cricket <u>jump</u> across the computer screen. ____hop____
7. Malik <u>laughed</u> when the cricket stopped and waved. __giggled__

Try It

1. Write a sentence using a synonym for the word **small**.
   Answers will vary.
2. Write a sentence using a synonym for the word **yelled**.
   Answers will vary.

Spectrum Language Arts
Grade 2

Chapter 3 Lesson 18
Usage
125

125

Lesson 3.19 Antonyms

NAME _____

An **antonym** is a word that means the opposite of another word. Here are some examples of antonyms.

big, little	old, young
happy, sad	first, last
right, wrong	never, always

Identify It

There are two antonyms in each sentence below. Circle each pair of antonyms.

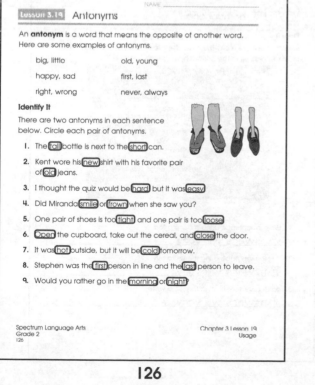

1. The (tall) bottle is next to the (short) can.
2. Kent wore his (new) shirt with his favorite pair of (old) jeans.
3. I thought the quiz would be (hard) but it was (easy)
4. Did Miranda (smile) or (frown) when she saw you?
5. One pair of shoes is too (tight) and one pair is too (loose)
6. (Open) the cupboard, take out the cereal, and (close) the door.
7. It was (hot) outside, but it will be (cold) tomorrow.
8. Stephen was the (first) person in line and the (last) person to leave.
9. Would you rather go in the (morning) or (night)

Spectrum Language Arts
Grade 2
126

Chapter 3 Lesson 19
Usage

126

Lesson 3.19 Antonyms

NAME _____

Solve It

In the spaces, write an antonym for each word below. Then, circle the antonyms in the word search puzzle. Words can be found across and down.

1. yell w_h_i_s_p_e_r
2. pull p_u_s_h
3. empty f_u_l_l
4. win l_o_s_e
5. yes n_o
6. love h_a_t_e
7. over u_n_d_e_r
8. down u_p

```
q  a  w  h  i  s  p  e  r  p
f  u  l  l  c  g  u  p  j  t
m  n  n  o  k  h  s  p  x  a
a  d  g  s  y  b  h  a  t  e
z  e  b  e  o  l  p  f  d  j
d  r  l  c  h  z  k  p  l  o
```

Try It

1. Write a sentence using an antonym for **loud**.
   Answers will vary.
2. Write a sentence using an antonym for **soft**.
   Answers will vary.

Spectrum Language Arts
Grade 2

Chapter 3 Lesson 19
Usage
127

127

Spectrum Language Arts
Grade 2

Answer Key

Page 128

Synonyms are words that have the same, or almost the same, meanings.

throw, toss	close, near
quick, fast	sad, unhappy
huge, giant	beautiful, pretty

Antonyms are words that mean the opposite of one another.

up, down	happy, sad
heavy, light	hot, cold
new, old	smooth, rough

Putting It Together

Read each pair of sentences. If the underlined words are synonyms, write **S** in the blank. If they are antonyms, write **A** in the blank.

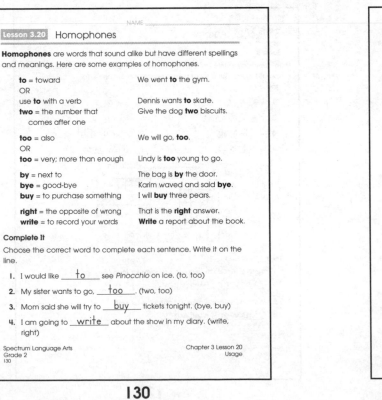

1. **A** Colby's puppet had <u>dark</u> hair.
   Nina's puppet had <u>light</u> hair.

2. **A** <u>First</u>, Colby painted a face on his puppet.
   The <u>last</u> thing Nina did was button her puppet's dress.

3. **S** Nina tied a <u>little</u> bow in her puppet's hair.
   Colby's puppet had a <u>small</u> frog in its pocket.

4. **S** "You did a <u>great</u> job painting your puppet's face," said Nina.
   "I think your puppet is <u>terrific</u>," said Colby.

Spectrum Language Arts
Grade 2
128
Review: Chapter 3 Lessons 18–19
Usage

128

Page 129

There is an antonym in the box for each underlined word. Write the antonyms above them.

below	same	few
huge	small	hard
sits	boring	outside

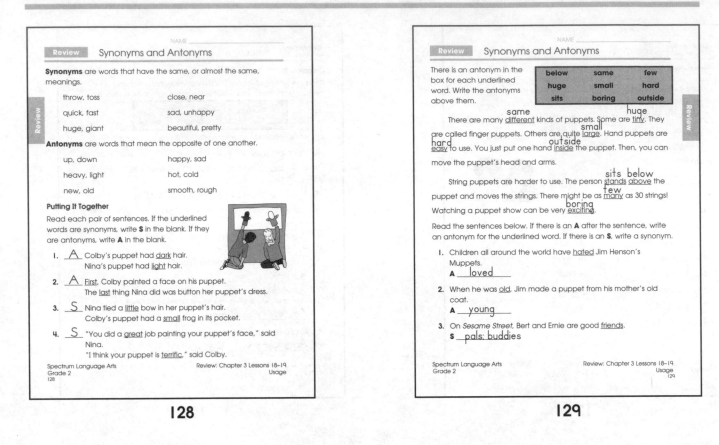

There are many <u>different</u> kinds of puppets. Some are <u>tiny</u>. They **same**   **huge**
are called finger puppets. Others are quite <u>large</u>. Hand puppets are **small**
<u>easy</u> to use. You just put one hand <u>inside</u> the puppet. Then, you can **hard**   **outside**
move the puppet's head and arms.

String puppets are harder to use. The person <u>stands</u> <u>above</u> the **sits below**
puppet and moves the strings. There might be as <u>many</u> as 30 strings! **few**
Watching a puppet show can be very <u>exciting</u>. **boring**

Read the sentences below. If there is an **A** after the sentence, write an antonym for the underlined word. If there is an **S**, write a synonym.

1. Children all around the world have <u>hated</u> Jim Henson's Muppets.
   A loved

2. When he was <u>old</u>, Jim made a puppet from his mother's old coat.
   A young

3. On *Sesame Street*, Bert and Ernie are good <u>friends</u>.
   S pals; buddies

Spectrum Language Arts
Grade 2
Review: Chapter 3 Lessons 18–19
Usage
129

129

Page 130

Homophones are words that sound alike but have different spellings and meanings. Here are some examples of homophones.

to = toward	We went **to** the gym.
OR	
use **to** with a verb	Dennis wants **to** skate.
two = the number that comes after one	Give the dog **two** biscuits.
too = also	We will go, **too**.
OR	
too = very; more than enough	Lindy is **too** young to go.
by = next to	The bag is **by** the door.
bye = good-bye	Karim waved and said **bye**.
buy = to purchase something	I will **buy** three pears.
right = the opposite of wrong	That is the **right** answer.
write = to record your words	**Write** a report about the book.

Complete It

Choose the correct word to complete each sentence. Write it on the line.

1. I would like ___to___ see *Pinocchio* on ice. (to, too)

2. My sister wants to go, ___too___. (two, too)

3. Mom said she will try to ___buy___ tickets tonight. (bye, buy)

4. I am going to ___write___ about the show in my diary. (write, right)

Spectrum Language Arts
Grade 2
130
Chapter 3 Lesson 20
Usage

130

Page 131

Proof It

Read the poster below. There are five mistakes. Cross out each mistake. Then, write the correct homophone above it.

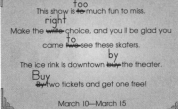

> Come see Pinocchio on ice!
> **too**
> This show is ~~to~~ much fun to miss.
> **right**
> Make the ~~write~~ choice, and you'll be glad you
> **to**
> came ~~two~~ see these skaters.
> **by**
> The ice rink is downtown ~~buy~~ the theater.
> **Buy**
> ~~By~~ two tickets and get one free!
>
> March 10—March 15

Try It

1. Write a sentence using the word **too**.
   Answers will vary.

2. Write a sentence using the word **buy**.
   Answers will vary.

3. Write a sentence using the word **write**.
   Answers will vary.

Spectrum Language Arts
Grade 2
Chapter 3 Lesson 20
Usage
131

131

Answer Key

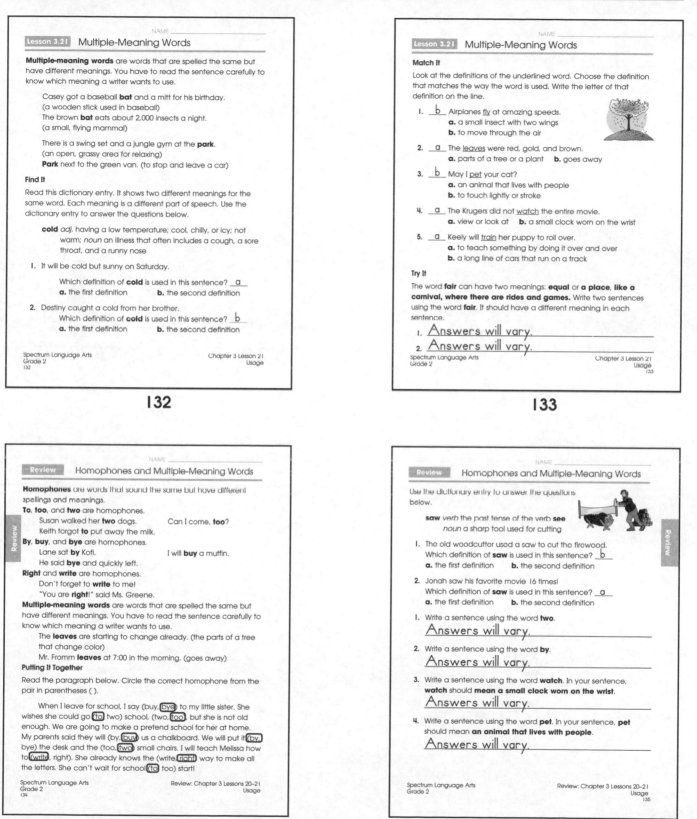

132

Lesson 3.21 Multiple-Meaning Words

Multiple-meaning words are words that are spelled the same but have different meanings. You have to read the sentence carefully to know which meaning a writer wants to use.

Casey got a baseball **bat** and a mitt for his birthday.
(a wooden stick used in baseball)
The brown **bat** eats about 2,000 insects a night.
(a small, flying mammal)

There is a swing set and a jungle gym at the **park**.
(an open, grassy area for relaxing)
Park next to the green van. (to stop and leave a car)

Find It

Read this dictionary entry. It shows two different meanings for the same word. Each meaning is a different part of speech. Use the dictionary entry to answer the questions below.

cold *adj.* having a low temperature; cool, chilly, or icy; not warm; *noun* an illness that often includes a cough, a sore throat, and a runny nose

1. It will be cold but sunny on Saturday.
   Which definition of **cold** is used in this sentence? __a__
   a. the first definition   **b.** the second definition

2. Destiny caught a cold from her brother.
   Which definition of **cold** is used in this sentence? __b__
   a. the first definition   **b.** the second definition

Spectrum Language Arts
Grade 2
132

Chapter 3 Lesson 21
Usage

133

Lesson 3.21 Multiple-Meaning Words

Match It

Look at the definitions of the underlined word. Choose the definition that matches the way the word is used. Write the letter of that definition on the line.

1. __b__ Airplanes <u>fly</u> at amazing speeds.
   a. a small insect with two wings
   b. to move through the air

2. __a__ The <u>leaves</u> were red, gold, and brown.
   a. parts of a tree or a plant   **b.** goes away

3. __b__ May I <u>pet</u> your cat?
   a. an animal that lives with people
   b. to touch lightly or stroke

4. __a__ The Krugers did not <u>watch</u> the entire movie.
   a. view or look at   **b.** a small clock worn on the wrist

5. __a__ Keely will <u>train</u> her puppy to roll over.
   a. to teach something by doing it over and over
   b. a long line of cars that run on a track

Try It

The word **fair** can have two meanings: **equal** or **a place, like a carnival, where there are rides and games.** Write two sentences using the word **fair**. It should have a different meaning in each sentence.

1. Answers will vary.
2. Answers will vary.

Spectrum Language Arts
Grade 2

Chapter 3 Lesson 21
Usage
133

134

Review Homophones and Multiple-Meaning Words

Homophones are words that sound the same but have different spellings and meanings.
To, **too**, and **two** are homophones.
   Susan walked her **two** dogs.   Can I come, **too**?
   Keith forgot **to** put away the milk.
By, **buy**, and **bye** are homophones.
   Lane sat **by** Kofi.   I will **buy** a muffin.
   He said **bye** and quickly left.
Right and **write** are homophones.
   Don't forget **to** **write** to me!
   "You are **right**!" said Ms. Greene.
Multiple-meaning words are words that are spelled the same but have different meanings. You have to read the sentence carefully to know which meaning a writer wants to use.
   The **leaves** are starting to change already. (the parts of a tree that change color)
   Mr. Fromm **leaves** at 7:00 in the morning. (goes away)

Putting It Together

Read the paragraph below. Circle the correct homophone from the pair in parentheses ( ).

When I leave for school, I say (buy, (bye)) to my little sister. She wishes she could go ((to) two) school, (two, (too)) but she is not old enough. We are going to make a pretend school for her at home. My parents said they will (by, (buy)) us a chalkboard. We will put it ((by) bye) the desk and the (too, (two)) small chairs. I will teach Melissa how to ((write), right). She already knows the (write, (right)) way to make all the letters. She can't wait for school ((to) too) start!

Spectrum Language Arts
Grade 2
134

Review: Chapter 3 Lessons 20–21
Usage

135

Review Homophones and Multiple-Meaning Words

Use the dictionary entry to answer the questions below.

saw *verb* the past tense of the verb **see**
   noun a sharp tool used for cutting

1. The old woodcutter used a saw to cut the firewood.
   Which definition of **saw** is used in this sentence? __b__
   a. the first definition   **b.** the second definition

2. Jonah saw his favorite movie 16 times!
   Which definition of **saw** is used in this sentence? __a__
   a. the first definition   **b.** the second definition

1. Write a sentence using the word **two**.
   Answers will vary.

2. Write a sentence using the word **by**.
   Answers will vary.

3. Write a sentence using the word **watch**. In your sentence, **watch** should **mean a small clock worn on the wrist**.
   Answers will vary.

4. Write a sentence using the word **pet**. In your sentence, **pet** should mean **an animal that lives with people**.
   Answers will vary.

Spectrum Language Arts
Grade 2

Review: Chapter 3 Lessons 20–21
Usage
135